The Four Levels of Reintegration

Building blocks for successful transition

Travis Centell Abercrombie

Dedication

This work is dedicated to all of my OutRight brothers from 2013-2019 with special recognition to:

Lee Nelson, Lester Young, Nykolos Peterson, Benjamin Green, Todd Bussey,

Benjamin P. Cornish, Rodney Horton, Darrell Moiser, Anthione (Kareem) Paden, and many others like:

Jarvis Johnson, Marcus Bynum, Rick Jordan, Chaplain Patoka and Doug Berryhill;

And to my three children:

Unique L. McKinney-Abercrombie

Sierra A. Abercrombie

Travis Abercrombie Jr.

For inspiring me to reach for higher aspirations even in their absence.

I also thank my Lord and Savior Jesus Christ of whom I am not ashamed and embody each and every day.

The Four Levels of Reintegration ©2020 is a product of *The Resurgence Post-Conviction Rehabilitation Program* (**RP²**)

*All quotes were created by the author unless otherwise stated by notation. Definitions provided throughout this workbook were taken from *Word Web* application download.

Four Levels of Reintegration Workbook

This workbook is presented to the following *RP²* participant in hope that it will greatly affect the degree to which they achieve success during and after transitioning back into society, family, and prominence:

NAME: ____

DATE: ____

TERM: ______________________________________

If this workbook is lost or misplaced please return it to the Resurgence Post-Conviction Rehabilitation Program or contact us online at RP2TA.SC@gmail.com

Introduction

The Four Levels of Reintegration is a four-dimensional concept that when continually addressed has the potential to produce a nucleus like result that has the power to hold together and sustain the efforts and successes of all who engage its applications.

Designed to be used after incarceration, it works best if the ex-offender has engaged any of the various rehab prep material out there. Notice I said it works best; the material is also useful to those who lacked even the minimum degree of rehabilitation.

The goal was to make this course easy and no nonsense. Ex-offenders have enough going on already with family, friends, employment, etc. and don't need to be burdened or oppressed by anything that is supposed to aide their transition efforts.

As is true with any material, this is not one size fits all. Though it will work for most; it won't work for everyone. Each ex-offender must find his/her own path to success and the aides that best fit with it. This material can either stand alone or compliment other source material.

Each level has been dissected according to its particular definition and application in each of the four dimensions. We tend to take words for granted or only use them in their simplest forms. However, a word can have many definitions as well as applications.

In this course the word *level* is the focus. In dimension one, level means to direct emphatically or forcefully toward someone/something. In level two, it means to tear down or raze; to knock down with or as with a blow. For dimension three it means to exhibit no abrupt variations; steady; rational and balanced—sensible. And lastly, in dimension four it is defined as a natural or proper position, place or stage; being of the same degree of rank, standing, or advantage as another; equal.

I have strived to draw from each of its definitions the proper application that I feel each ex-offender needs to grasp and apply out in the real world. This material creates for any willing ex-offender the ability to reverse most of the effects of their past offences.

Engage the course. Learn from your mistakes and have fun in the process. I wish you luck.

Respectfully,

Travis C. Abercrombie

Author; Founder of
Resurgence Post-Conviction Rehabilitation Program

*RP*²

Level 1 defined: To direct emphatically or forcefully toward someone.

Dimensional application: Dealing with the consequences leveled against you because of incarceration.

Dimension: Residual effects of confinement (after release)

Points of focus:

A. Hybrid behaviors

Vocab

Hybrid: A composite of mixed origin

Behavior – the aggregate of the responses, reactions or movements made by an organism in any situation; The action or reaction of something under specified circumstances

Consequence - The outcome of an event especially as relative to an individual

Getting released from prison challenges us in different ways. One way in particular, is by creating hybrid behaviors to compensate for our lack of preparation for societal living.

We take one behavior, like using the restroom, and we integrate it with the prison culture resulting in: flushing the toilet 20 or more times (in one sitting). However, when we max-out we find it hard to break the behavior.

The behavior may not be bad in and of itself; the difference is we don't pay for water in prison, but in society we do. How many of your relatives would strongly criticize your new habit of wasting water?

What would you say if you were the one paying for the water?

As an ex-offender you must go to great lengths to make sure that the behaviors you're taking to society—belong in society.

Don't think that people will understand that you're in transition. Cut away the baggage before it cost you more than you are willing to pay.

In the space below list the hybrid behaviors you can recognize in your life.

1)	2)
3)	4)
5)	6)
7)	8)
9)	10)
11)	12)

The goal is to make these undesired behaviors your focal point. Once they have your attention, you must do two things:

1. *Stop practicing the behavior in question*
2. *Discover it's opposite and begin the application process*

Simply knowing what the behavior is or being tired of the consequences of the behavior—is not enough. It has to be stopped. Now, you should also be aware of this fact: *just because you have stopped a particular behavior does not mean that you have also negated its consequence.*

Ex: Imagine that someone has just done you wrong. You confront them about the issue and they claim that they will never do it again. What then happens with the consequence of their wrong doing? Does it go away? Of course not. The natural consequence whatever the action is now in play.

What then can be done about one's prior *bad behaviors* and *consequences*?

Every individual has the ability (*after the fact*) to influence the degree to which a natural consequence is enforced upon them and others.

Ex. Your child telling you he/she wrecked the car vs. you finding out they wrecked the car *influences the degree of consequence.* Taking a guilty plea because of damning evidence vs. choosing to go to trial (in spite of) *influences the degree of the consequence.*

What you do in response to your hybrid behaviors is just as important, if not in some cases more important than the initial behavior itself.

B. The loss of desired relationships

Due to some of those behaviors discussed in the last section and our prior convictions, we have lost or greatly damaged many of our personal relationships.

These relationships range from but are not limited to: *family, friends, community, religious networks, and even employment.*

Some effects are obvious; others not so much. Now that you realize there is a way to affect the consequences of your actions and that you can alter the degree to which it is implied—you have a choice to make.

Which relationships must be addressed first? Which ones do you value most? Which, if neglected would have the greatest effect on your transition?

At this time, in the space below list your most important relationships from greatest to least.

(Greatest being 1; Least being 6)

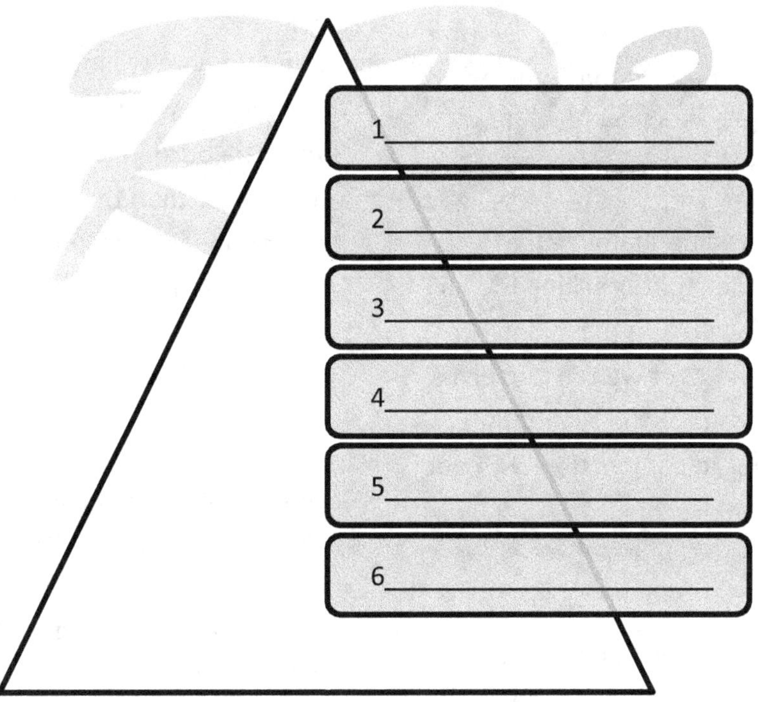

Alright what are you willing to do to combat the effects of your behaviors on your greatest relationship; what about your least? Why is this important?

As an ex-offender, you must understand that you can't do it all now that you're out. You must have priorities to help guide you in where you spend your time and efforts.

Ex. You can't put the relationship between you and your children at 1 if you spend more time working (60-80 hours) trying to get back the things you used to have. Or you can't put religious faith at 6 if you actually want it to be worth more than words.

Your priorities **must** match up with the time and effort you put forth continually.

The lack of consistency in this area probably brought you to the point of incarceration in the first place.

Think tick-tack-toe. The goal is a straight line of sight from priorities to efforts; from efforts to desired results.

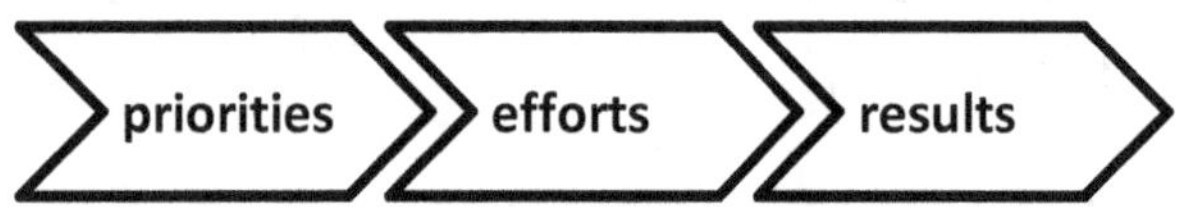

Like many others, you may come to see that what you say you value a lot may only be a little and what you are believed to value least—you value more than imagined.

For instance, if you valued family at a 1, would you really think that breaking the law and going to prison was your best/only option? Of course not. Yet we tell ourselves things like this to assuage the reality that we are not behaving in conjunction with our values.

Vocab

Cognitive dissonance - psychological conflict resulting from incongruous beliefs and attitudes held simultaneously.

This is what happens every time you or I behave contrary to what we sell to others on a daily basis. We advertise consistency but find we are only consistent in being inconsistent.

If we are to make it in society and become successful in any facet of life we have to start bridging the gap between who we are and who we want to be.

All relationships are built on trust. Without it love will wane and the relationship will be unsuccessful and volatile. This is for any relationship.

The area of rebuilding relationships is one of the hardest any of us will have to deal with because our lives are so interconnected with the lives of others. There is always to sides to consider; always another view to see.

What you are willing to offer your children may not be what they actually desire from you. The burden you place on yourself may be heavier than the one your wife is presenting. The future you see may be dimmer than what your employer sees in you. So many different relationships, so many fields of play—you can't just be haphazard.

Find out what is expected of you and what others expect of you before you begin fixing the relationship. If you apply the right solution to the wrong problem, you will get the same result as if you had done nothing at all.

C. Declassification by society

The moment you were convicted you were also demoted in class. You were no longer the law-abiding citizen so willfully promoted by society.

Vocab

Citizen - A native or naturalized member of a state or other political community.

Lawful - Having a legally established claim; Authorized, sanctioned by, or in accordance with law.

Being a lawful member of society is the standard. Whether others do it is not the issue; whether or not you do it is. It doesn't matter about the ones who got away—if you are the one who got caught.

Most times, society will not give you a second chance if you refuse to take responsibility for your actions. The law of the land is the law of the land; your opinions and feelings are secondary.

Alright, so all this is important to know because with citizenship comes rights; the violation of that citizenship will result in the loss of or restriction to any number of those rights.

Ex. As a law-abiding-citizen, you have the freedom to come and go as you please within whichever state you reside; however, when you fail to be a law-abiding-citizen and are convicted—your freedom can be revoked for however long your state deems fit.

In most cases we are choosing to be declassed by society, yet we will rail on them for punishing our bad behavior. What sense that makes I don't know, but we must refrain from this mind-set if we seek re-classification after release.

In a later section we will discuss the value of our classification. They say, "You never know what you had until it's gone." This is true in regards to our classification and rights as a citizen.

In the space provided below, list some other rights/privileges that you took for granted in the commission of your crime:

Rights/Privileges

1.______________________________

2.______________________________

3.______________________________

4.______________________________

5.______________________________

6.______________________________

7.______________________________

My goal is not to make you depressed, but to allow you the opportunity to see things from your family's or society's perspective. The results of your work in this level are *reality*.

You have to determine for yourself whether or not you will live in reality or keep daydreaming in your own little *fairytale*.

Vocab

Declassify – to lift the restriction on and make available again (or for the first time)

Reclassify - Classify anew, change the previous classification

Every time someone violates the law of the land the protection from the consequences of the law are lifted and the individual is made susceptible again or for the first time to those consequences.

Contrariwise, if that same person is successful in dealing with those consequences, repentant of the infractions, and willing to conform to the standard of living set by the state—the state is then required to give back (reclassify) the original status of citizenship and accompanying rights.

It will take more effort to regain your rights and full citizenship than it did for you to lose them. That effort is multiplied with every subsequent violation on your part.

Truth is you may not even care what society says about you or how they class you. That's all good, however, those with whom you have to interact with for work and networking may see things differently. So even if you don't care—act like you do.

D. Little to no work history

What is and what isn't work history tends to vary depending on who you ask. I believe it is all in explanation and wording.

Vocab

Transferable - Capable of being moved or conveyed from one place to another

Work History – a record that depicts all past, current, and ongoing occupations for which you received payment (Often used to determine employment risk, employee commitment level, and wages)

Employable - Physically and mentally capable of working at a regular job and available

Work history is another way of saying work experience. With this in mind, my philosophy is that the same job skills that apply in society apply in prison.

If the only issue is location—you have no issue. If you can run a prison cafeteria, this is experience for the food industry. If you were a teacher's aide, then you apply to help in adult education. A no is only final if you accept it as such.

The skills learned during your incarceration can and will be used outside of prison; if not by you, then by someone else.

"Opportunity may only knock once; she is sometimes impatient."

Alright, so in the spaces provided, state your work history from before prison, in prison, and potential employment now that you are out of prison:

Work History (Before Prison)

1. ______________________
2. ______________________
3. ______________________
4. ______________________
5. ______________________
6. ______________________
7. ______________________
8. ______________________
9. ______________________

History of Work (Prison)

1. ______________________
2. ______________________
3. ______________________
4. ______________________
5. ______________________
6. ______________________
7. ______________________
8. ______________________
9. ______________________

Potentail Employment/Employers

1 _______________________

2 _______________________

3 _______________________

4 _______________________

5 _______________________

6 _______________________

7 _______________________

8 _______________________

9 _______________________

When you have little to no work history to work with you have to create history. Do so without lying though. Nothing says "I don't want employment" more than a lie on an application.

When I say be creative, I mean tell the truth, but in a way that people will be interested in what you have to offer.

Ex. Simply saying you were a kitchen worker on an application won't get you hired at Longhorn Steak House; however, saying you were a second line meal cook for approx. 1500 people per day—sounds like you know what you're doing. Get my point?

"Experience is important to employers only if it is first important to the employee."

In order to be creative in the sense promoted in this material you must be knowledgeable of the particular skills you are trying to sell to employers. In the space below, list each transferable skill that you

have learned working in prison:

☐ <u>Transferable skills</u>

☐ _______________________

☐ _______________________

☐ _______________________

☐ _______________________

☐ _______________________

☐ _______________________

☐ _______________________

☐ _______________________

For every transferable skill you have—there is a potential job out here waiting for you to apply. What are you waiting for?

E. The need for rehabilitation

Why rehab?

Why not?

You may be thinking that you are good as you are and now that you've completed your sentence, you're home-free. Wrong.

It's a known fact that individuals who need rehabilitation the most—can't see that they need it. This is why it is so important to have truthfully outspoken people in your circle.

Vocab

Rehabilitate - Help to readapt, as to a former state of health or good repute. Restore to a state of good condition or operation.

Purge - The act of clearing yourself (or another) from some stigma or charge. An act of removing by cleansing; ridding of sediment or other undesired elements.

What you have experienced by being incarcerated, being removed from your family, being defamed because of your actions, and being punished without being offered a structure/blueprint to be better— is abnormal.

Though everything I have said thus far in previous sections is true, we have to consider the human factor in this.

It seems as if society wants you to be better without their aide. You committed the crime by yourself, so they have designed an incomplete prison system that forces you to engage the rehabilitation process by yourself as well.

This is mentioned as a fact; not an excuse. You have to do what is right by all parties: family, friends, yourself, and society—in spite of the human factor; in spite of the incomplete prison system.

They don't owe you anything; you don't owe them anything; you owe yourself everything.

When it comes to rehab, society will reap its benefits; however, the greatest benefit of all goes to you. Rehab is what you make it and what you want it to be. You have to fully engage the process to be successful in every other aspect of your life.

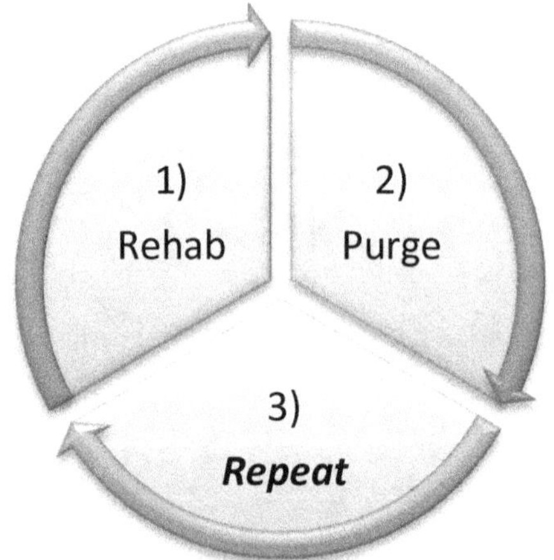

As you see, the process is continual; not a one-time solution. After prison you will never stop being different, people will never stop wanting you to be the same, and so you should not be alright with either. After prison, better should always be the goal, because without rehab—you can always get worse.

It is in the rehabilitation phase of living that you begin to remove hybrid behaviors like those described earlier. Just thinking about the consequences of not rehabbing should push you to get a better understanding of rehabbing.

Rehabilitating yourself allows for the purging process to take place. As you get healthier mentally and social-emotionally you will start to discover the lowering degree by which people judge you for your past mistakes. Sometimes all it takes is a little initiative on your part to show those around you that you actually care about your future.

"People tend to help those who help themselves first; not the other way around."

However, the fact still remains that you must realize your need for this. Rehab can't be forced on anyone. The more it is forced, the more it will be refused.

Remember you are choosing rehabilitation for you *directly* and for others *indirectly*.

What is it going to be?

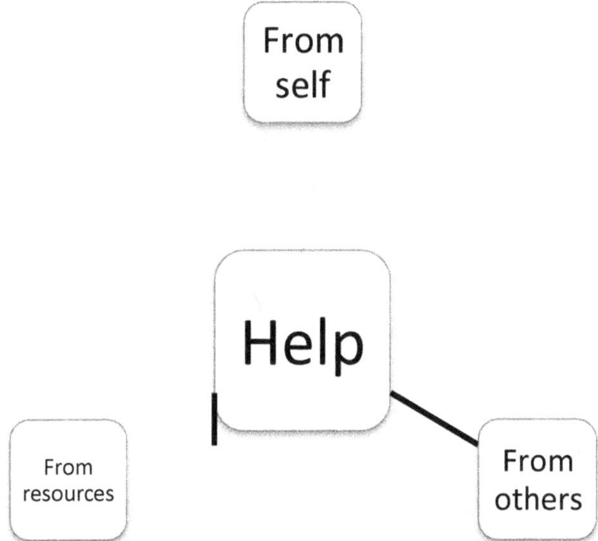

Level 2 defined: To tear down or raze. To knock down with or as with a blow.

Dimensional application: Tearing down who you were and establishing the foundation of who you are becoming.

Dimension: Reinvention of the offender

Points of focus:

A. Defining a better standard of living

In order to define a better way of living, it might be best to know what didn't work with the old way of living.

Luckily for you we have already covered a few areas of your old way of doing things and you are starting to come around to a clearer perception of things.

When defining this new standard, you must consider the different aspects of your life. This is important because certain things may change in one aspect but not the other.

What areas can you think of that may call for different actions or reactions? Are there areas in which the same action or reaction would be appropriate?

Vocab

Standard - A basis for comparison; a reference point against which other things can be evaluated; the ideal in terms of which something can be judged.

Displace - Cause to move, usually with force or pressure; Take the place of or have precedence over; Cause to move or shift into a new position or place, both in a concrete and in an abstract sense

Replace - Put in the place of another; switch seemingly equivalent items; Take the place or move into the position of; Substitute a person or thing for (another that is broken or inefficient or lost or no longer working or yielding what is expected)

We have to set/discover a new standard before we start making changes. Your standard determines what needs to go and what needs to stay. Who needs to be in your life and who should *kick rocks*? What comes into play?

Consider your goals, your past, your support system, and even the environment you will be returning to.

Your new standard will influence each of these at different degrees. It is your job to make sure that no matter what must go or what must stay, there is balance. Without it you will only have devastation and your chances at helpful and successful transitioning will be minimized.

Look at it this way. Imagine you got dressed before checking the weather and walked outside into 101 degrees. After you retreat back into the house, you stand in front of the mirror and try to decide what you will keep on and what you will take off.

Developing a new standard of living is pretty much the same: you have to consider the conditions before making any permanent decisions.

With every choice you make—either to keep/remove—you are tearing down how you seen yourself in the past, how you see yourself in the present, and how you want to see yourself in the future. Every decision matters and *no decision is irrelevant.*

"…let every man take heed how he buildeth thereupon."

-1 Corinthians 3:10

Be careful about whose advice you heed after release. Not everyone is a well-wisher. Any advice must be viewed through your desired standard of living and the aspirations associated with it.

The biggest thing we have to keep in mind when forming our foundation/standard of living is that others will build upon it/suffer from it later. The amount of consideration and proper application in this area will determine what happens down the line.

So how serious are you about becoming better? Are you really tired of who you were or who you have become? What steps did you take in prison to change yourself (good/bad)?

Displace and replace

Anything that you displace from your foundation must be consciously replaced with something better and appropriate. Failing to be intentional during the replacement process leaves the door open for the same behaviors or conditions to re-root or overgrow into other areas of your foundation.

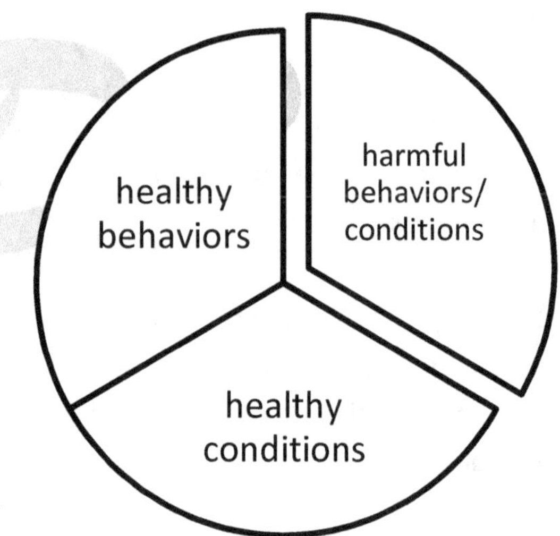

As you see in the pie chart above, harmful behaviors and conditions have been displaced from the healthy behaviors and conditions; however, once you displace these you have to graft in a proper replacement: healthy reinforcement.

Vocab

Reinforcement - An act performed to strengthen approved behavior.

Healthy - Promoting health; healthful. Exercising or showing good judgment.

Healthy reinforcement should promote and strengthen the application of healthy and approved behavior that is based on good judgment.

Anyone or anything that you are using for reinforcement should meet this standard. If not, even these should be removed and replaced. Doing so ensures the security of your new foundation or standard. Take a look at the revised pie chart below.

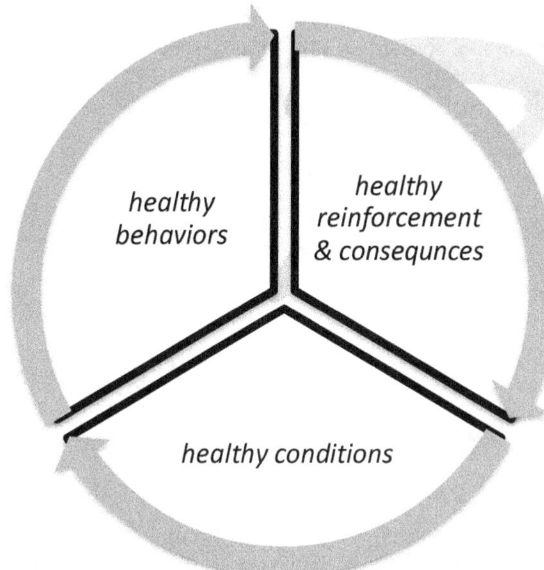

As you see, once you replace the harmful behaviors and conditions with healthy reinforcement a clear and continuous cycle is formed. This cycle, once formed, can withstand minor lapses of judgment or inconsistencies if immediately addressed by you.

Your failure, however, to:

- Address recurring unhealthy behaviors
- Combat unhealthy conditions

- Adhere to healthy reinforcement
- Learn from healthy consequences
- Remove harmful things or people who may threaten the health or successful formation of your new standard or foundation

will soon enough break the continuous current that holds together the cycle.

So how do you know when you have successfully replaced a harmful behavior?

There are no absolutes in this area; however, if the following can be said about you then you can rest assured:

✓ The harmful behavior is no longer an unconscious behavior
✓ You can associate your current behavior with your current standard of living
✓ You (after consistent application) have begun to experience the fruit of healthy behavior
✓ And your people of positive re-enforcement have given confirmation of the changed behavior

The hardest thing in this area will be replacing the right behaviors and replacing them properly.

Displacing the wrong behavior too early may lead to a breakdown in the inception of the desired one.

Make an effort to educate yourself on any and every behavior that you displace and infix into your living cycle.

Not knowing the consequences or rewards of these behaviors could be calamitous for you and those who have attached themselves to you.

"A failure to educate oneself before action leads to casualties in action."

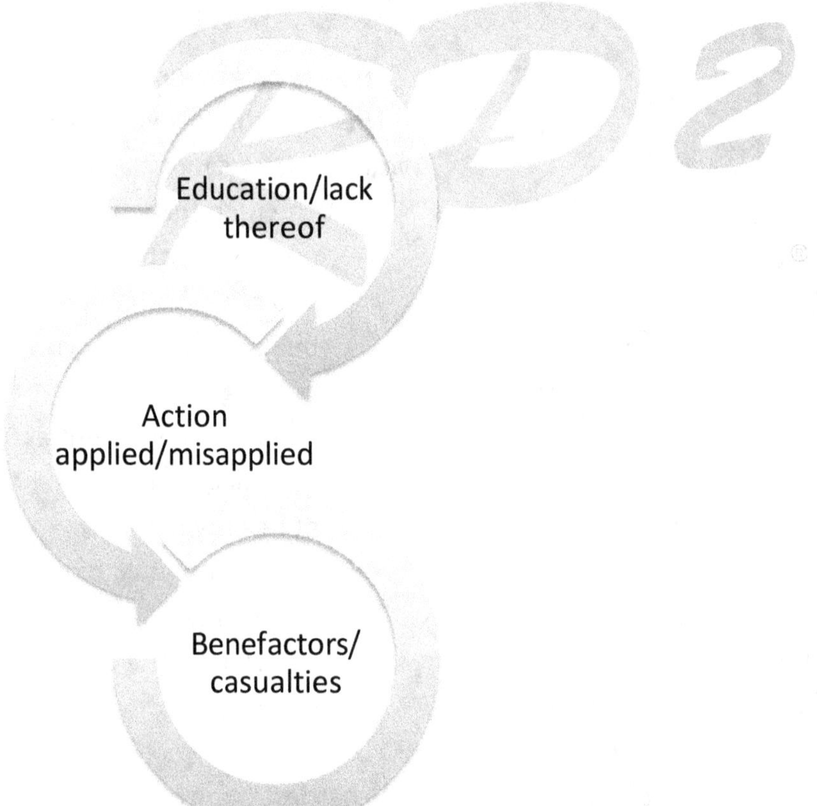

B. Forgiving inwardly before expecting it outwardly

With certain things action must take place within before it can be recognized without. Forgiveness is one of those things.

"The weak can never forgive. Forgiveness is the attribute of the strong."

-Mahatma Gandhi

Vocab

Forgiveness - Compassionate feelings that support a willingness to forgive; the act of excusing a mistake or offense.

Reconciliation - The reestablishing of cordial relations; getting two things to correspond.

As an ex-offender, it would be wise to understand that forgiveness can be granted *without* the guarantee of a continued relationship.

Most times we believe our family and friends are obligated to renew a relationship with us on the basis of forgiveness; however, forgiveness involves supporting feelings of the act itself. **No relationship required**.

Are you prepared to deal with this reality? How many relationships have you damaged through harmful behavior?

Have you apologized and asked for forgiveness of those actions? Or are you expecting something for nothing?

This explanation is universal. It's the same in society as a whole. If you commit a crime, you have brought damage to the relationship shared between you and the society at large. You are now in their debt. A penance must be paid and attached to that is forgiveness.

You were first to offend and so you must be first to make amends. This does not repair the relationship; it does, however, make known the rift that you have created.

This is because attached to your wrong doing is the loss of trust. The forgiveness is for the misdeed only. To create or repair a relationship, you must rebuild the trust that was removed by your actions.

This takes time and you have no control over how long it will take to rebuild that trust; that power belongs to the offended.

Now the silver lining is this:
- ❖ You have the power to forgive yourself and move on
- ❖ You have the ability to encourage forgiveness from others when your consistent actions require it
- ❖ You have the privilege of moving on with your life and becoming who you want to be—*in spite of the un-forgivingness of others*

Don't get me wrong, forgiveness is important. The problem is that the importance is highly determined by you. Some people find it hard to move on and become better people because mother, friend, girlfriend, or community can't get past their mistakes of the past.

In the end, as long as you forgive yourself and move past your own failures, nothing can stand in the way of your future.

The goal here is to put yourself in a position where you can determine which relationships are: *worth saving, worth creating, and worth enduring the consequences of.*

Don't burden yourself unnecessarily.

Vocab

Guilt - The state of having committed an offense. Remorse caused by feeling responsible for some offense

Guilt can cause us to keep relationships we would otherwise rid ourselves of. We understand that we have hurt someone outside of ourselves, but fail to understand that our friends and loved ones don't have the right to hold us in contempt for past actions.

Once you forgive yourself and others offer/refuse their forgiveness—it's over. There is nothing afterwards but your future. Do the same thing they're going to do: move on.

"The only way the past can hold us back is if we are failing to move on."

At this time, you will be required to write a letter to yourself, your family, and the society that you will be going back to. Use the space provided for all three:

To myself

____

____

____

____

____

____

____

____

____

____

_______________________________________.

Sincerely,
Self

To my family

____

____

____

____

____

____

____

____

____

____

____

____

____

____.

Sincerely,
Me

To my community/society

____

____

____

____

____

____

____

____

____

____

____

____.

Respectfully,
Fellow citizen

Mean what you say in these letters. Let them be for you a guidepost to the freedom of forgiveness and openness.

You don't have to stay in this closet of fear and un-forgiveness. You don't have to lose out on meaningful relationships. You can be repentant and guilt free. It's your choice—yours alone.

What's it going to be?

C. Creating and prioritizing goals

Alright, you're out of prison and must get your life in order. What will you do? Where will you go? For how long will you do it? What must happen for you to be successful at this job?

A lot of questions, right? Priorities are normally like that. There is no one-step success plan. Life doesn't work like that—anywhere.

Vocab

Priorities - Status established in order of importance or urgency

Goal (s) - The state of affairs that a plan is intended to achieve and that (when achieved) terminates the behavior intended to achieve it; the place designated as the end (as of a race or journey)

You may be thinking I don't need goals; I live in the moment. I live for today. I can make things work.

Most of us pretend to have it all figured out—until we don't. Bills are due. Our children need clothes. Something must be done.

Again, what do you do? When there are no goals for success and no priorities that drive them, how do you know that you have reached your mark?

Staying out of prison is a goal. However, what priorities will make you stay true? Being a good father is a goal. What priorities will help you be successful?

When deciding what your goals will be, you have to consider all aspects of your life; who you are. What constant or necessary roles do you engage in from day to day. Then after you've listed the roles, start to determine the goals and prioritize them in order of importance/time restraints. For example,

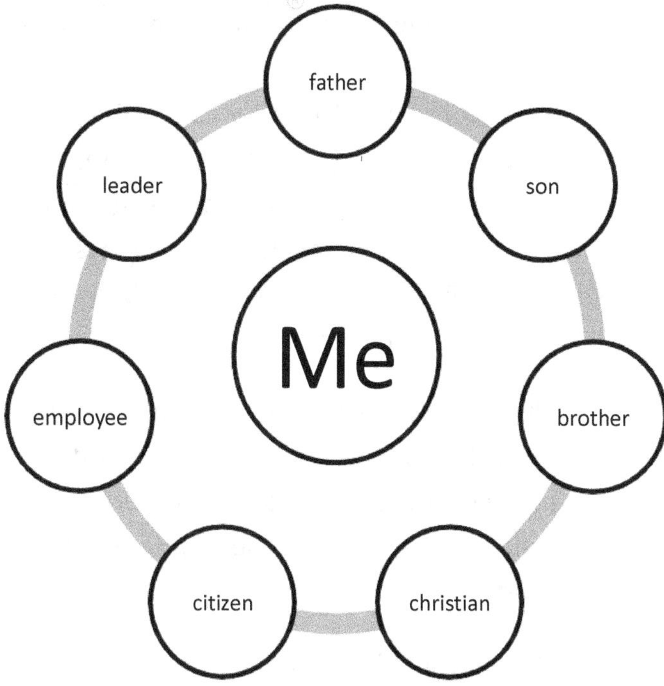

I would have to evaluate each of these roles in my life and create goals for them. My goals are determined by what each individual role requires for success.

So, as a:

- ✓ Father, I want to educate my children on all aspects of life; I want to create for them a challenging and nurturing environment to live; I want to be involved in the *big moments* of their lives.
- ✓ Son, I want to encourage my mother to be the best version of herself; provide for her the opportunity to experience things she bypassed earlier in life; make her proud of me as a man.
- ✓ Brother, remain a dependable outlet for advice, monetary aid, and empathy; strive to push them to achieve higher goals for themselves by doing the same; be a living example for my nieces and nephews to follow.
- ✓ Christian, live out what I claim to believe in public and in private; inspire others with my lifestyle and not my words only; forgive myself and others on a continual basis; remain steadfast.

Alright so you get the point. Don't just blow through this area; take the time to write it the right way so that you can get the right results in the end. Goal descriptions may be short/long-term.

The next step is putting things in order of importance:

1. Christian
2. Father
3. Son

4. Brother
5. Citizen
6. Employee/employer
7. Leader

Your order should demonstrate what roles are most important to you and cascade into the next role. When we get the first role in order, the foundation for the next has already been laid.

"Just as success in one area can impact the next; failure in an area can impact the rest."

Time for you to try. In the space provided, list every role that you currently play in your life:

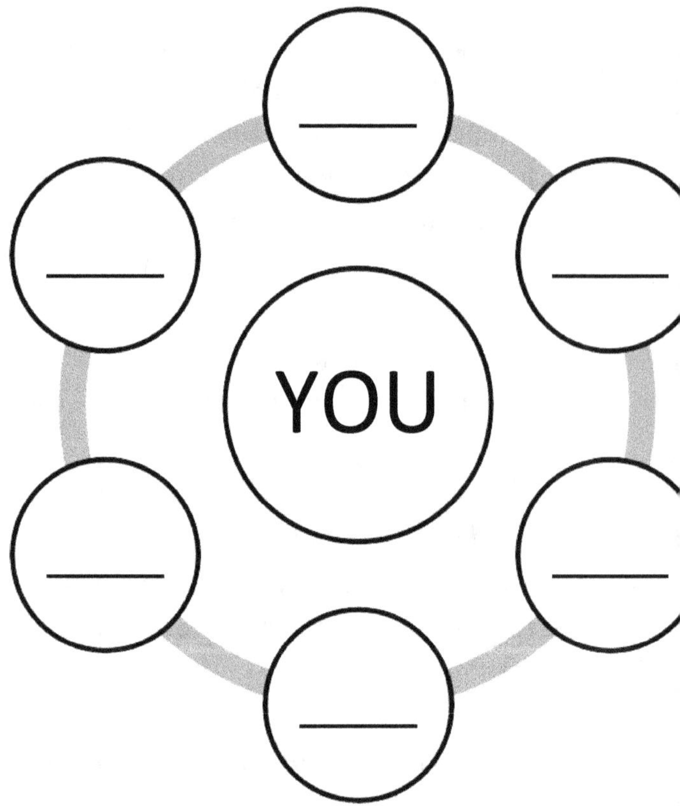

Now take each role and put them in order
from most important to least important:

1. _______________________
2. _______________________
3. _______________________
4. _______________________
5. _______________________
6. _______________________

Alright, now take each individual role and
describe the goals that you want attached
to them (for you to be successful in that
role). Write the role on the black line
(running up and down); write each
description on one of the three lines
provided:

(Example)

Once completed, you will have a guideline
to help you along the way and keep you on
a constant path to progress.

*"The effort you put in for
preparation and application will
fix the value of the results you
collect."*

(*see exercise 2.1 in the extras section)

D. Curbing unwanted habits or behaviors

What does it mean to curb a behavior/habit? Can we do it ourselves or do we need a specialist?

As we explained before we are in control of both our behaviors and habits as it pertains to our choices.

Vocab

Curb - Lessen the intensity of; temper; hold in restraint; hold or keep within limits; to put down by force or authority; Place restrictions on.

Context - The set of facts or circumstances that surround a situation or event

Consistency - Logical coherence and accordance with the facts

Not all behaviors are necessarily bad; some in the right context can be used to the benefit of all involved. The key, however, is your ability or willingness to be consistent within whichever context you apply them in.

As ex-offenders, we are not judged by whether we do the right things; we are judged on whether we do the right things on a consistent basis.

Anger would be a good example of something needing to be curbed in accordance to context. You may be angry at your child for disobeying something you told them to do; however, you typically won't let your anger harm the relationship. Typically.

Retaliation would be another. In prison, retaliation is a must when:

- Someone tries you in public settings
- Someone questions what you stand for/represent
- Someone puts their hands on you to bring harm
- Someone speaks to you in a profane manner

I could go on but you get the point, right? These same stimuli, in another context, call for you to curb your natural/learned responses.

You can't *shoot da one* with everyone in society who refuses to see things your way, or says something to you that you don't like. You will be in jail before you can explain the situation—and who wants that?

The key to being better in this area rests on the innate ability each of us have from our youth: *the ability to adapt.*

In prison, jail, or groups that are headed to one or both, we adapt/curb any habits and behaviors that the context would frown upon. The problem here, however, is that we do this even at the expense of who we are and who we want to be. *Public opinion is a heck of a motivator.*

In this lesson, your goal is to use the same motivation to lead you to do the right thing and enjoy the benefits of rightly applied behavior.

"Who we are in our most intimate relationships is who we are in everyday living; we must change before society catches up with those relationships."

Another motivator would be: your goals and values. These should always be at the forefront of your mind stimulating you to conform to any context without over-relaxing your standards of living.

In some cases, you can keep your old friends who are not currently aligned with the new you; however, with the condition that they refrain from the unwanted behavior around you. Remember this is not true for all cases.

Be the resistance

It is said that a little leaven will permeate the whole lump of dough. With this in mind, resolve to have none of it around you. Unwanted behaviors and habits that is.

In this area zero tolerance is an understatement. Every time you choose to engage and old way of doing things or allow others to indulge in those habits around you—your future is at stake. What you could lose in a matter of moments, could take you forever to regain.

This lesson forces you to apply what you learned in the previous one about your roles and goals. The facts that you have attributed to them now become the foundation of your consistency.

"What may seem difficult in the moment can have greater bearing on your future."

Every day you should be striving to be in (logical) coherence and accordance with the facts of those relationships you hold so dear.

The consistency is what will bring you success both in your personal and interpersonal relationships. Don't take it for granted; the price is too great.

E. Committing to the rehab process

Of course, you don't need rehab; you haven't been gone that long. You're not *shot out* like some of the people you know. *Are you*?

Vocab

Rehab - The restoration of someone to a useful place in society; vindication of a person's character and the re-establishment of that person's reputation

Ex-offenders have the wrong idea when it comes to rehab; as do many correctional institutions. I was in that group until I studied it for myself, engaged the process, and began to reap the benefits of *rehab.*

Rehab, contrary to popular opinion, is a choice. A choice made within the individual who desires rehab. It is not the job of the institution per se to force it upon unwilling participants.

No matter the amount of force, an unwilling individual will remain the same or become worse—not understanding the importance of rehab.

Rehab promotes the ability to restore an individual to a useful place in society. Because it is for the individual.

Though the society at large will no doubt reap benefits along the way, the rehab is for the individual (primarily).

Vocab

Restore - Restore by replacing a part or putting together what is torn or broken

Typically, this word is use to confirm bringing something or someone to its previous usable or working function; however, the definition I have chosen better fits the job at hand.

Why would anyone being released from confinement want to go back to the person they were before prison? I know it sounds good when we say it, but it is simply flawed thinking.
Why? Well it's simple. The person we were before coming to prison was:
- ✓ Still headed to prison
- ✓ Still ignorant of the consequences of past and currently engaged behaviors/habits
- ✓ Without the correction and knowledge of self that should come from actually engaging one's incarceration
- ✓ Unaware of empathy and the part it plays in the commission of a criminal offense

Now, why would you or I want that? Who would that benefit? It reminds me of a bad sequel of *Déjà vu*. Living life over and over thinking that *surely I've been here before.*

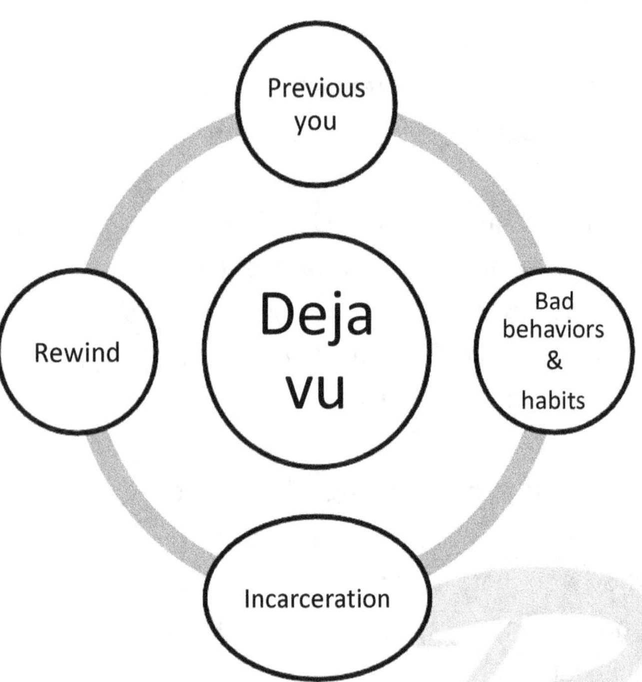

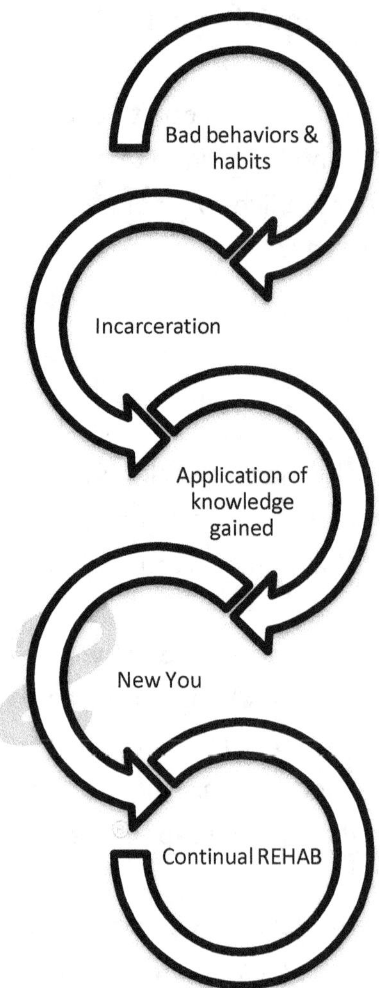

No, what we need is to somehow use our hindsight, lessons learned, new standards, and incarceration experience to pinpoint and replace parts of the cycle itself. This is restoration. **This is rehab**.

Without the process of replacement, the cycle can't be broken. This is why men and women max-out of prison only to return again. They have not redefined or fixed that which is clearly broken.

"You can't mend a broken heart without adding something new and you can't overcome recidivism without removing something old."

Your process should look something like this: ***removal of*** the previous you, and the option of rewinding; the ***addition of*** what you've already learned, the reformation of self, and the option to continually rehab that self.

Vindication of character and re-establishment of reputation can only come from such a process. *Don't fool yourself otherwise.*

Vocab

Vindication - The act of vindicating or defending against criticism or censure etc.

Re-establish - Restoration to a previous state

When you properly enact the process of rehab, you gain the right to have your newly created character defended by your accompanying body of work. Also, you place yourself in position to benefit from a reputation that you only pretended to have/had no knowledge of before.

Without rehab, your character is shot; your reputation is non-existent or a fairytale.

For you to be vindicated something has to change in you and be perceived by others around you. You simply cannot do this for yourself.

Your past may be riddled with criminal behavior, consequences of that behavior, and a path of destroyed relationships. Over time, when you chose a different path—new character, new relationships, penitence, empathy, and wisdom—you will be granted vindication by those who have the ability to do so.

You do not get to dictate when this takes place. God may vindicate you faster than society will, but with persistence and continual rehab society won't be far behind.

F. Recognizing where I am and what I can do about it

Things would probably be a lot better if you were not a convicted felon; however, the cards that you hold are simply different than those of others around you.

It's true that you cannot change your cards, but you can dictate how you use them. You can still be a winner—if you play your cards right.

Vocab

Location - A determination of the place where something/someone is

Support system - A network of facilities and people who interact and remain in informal communication for mutual assistance; a network that enables you to live in a certain style

Resilient - Recovering readily from adversity, depression, or the like

Where are you? No really, where are you physically? Why are you there? What opportunities are here, that can't be found elsewhere?

Your location after prison is so important, that making the wrong choice could place a ceiling upon your success that would otherwise not be there.

For instance, do you know how many convicted felons live in your area? Or how many jobs exist for such people? Have you even considered it? If not, start doing so, because the demographics and restraints in place will hinder you greatly if indeed you are ignorant of their effects.

When we were in prison, what we could and couldn't do was determined by which dorm we lived in. Some dorms had privileges that others did not, and if you wanted those privileges you had to relocate to the other dorms or change your environment—and the people in it.

While changing one's environment sounds noble and selfless; it is not always realistic. It goes back to priorities and sacrifice: what could you do now that will bring you closer to what you want later.

Location, location, location. If you have returned to an area that lacks the job diversity that you need, move. If you have returned to an area that is not conducive to the changes you have made in your life, move. If you know that people are willing to help you elsewhere—hello—move. Enough said?

Now, to your support system: who makes it up? Your old friends who want the old you back are of no help to you in this area. New friends who may only want a free ride on your coattail will only hold you back. You need support; not anchors.

Your support system should be comprised of people and resources that are favorable to your new ambitions and new way of thinking. Who comes to mind? Why them? If someone comes to mind and you don't want to use them but can't think of a reason why—ask yourself, why not them?

Caution! Family members that you know will be there for you regardless should be excluded for the moment. Think of those who can take you to the next level; people who can look at your past and your future objectively to determine the best way to help you. It may be a good idea to find those who won't go for your bull crap either.

"People who interact and remain in informal communication for mutual assistance…" Who fits this description? If you want to make it, now that you are out of prison, you must scrutinize anyone who says they can help but can never be reached. Or someone who says they understand your situation but only places unrealistic burdens upon you.

Examples of people to add to your support system are:

- ❖ Volunteers from prison
- ❖ Other inmates from prison who did the hard work while still on the inside
- ❖ Ex-offenders who have gotten out of prison and become productive citizens of their community and been out a year/better
- ❖ Members of the community/church that are willing to pour into you the tools that you need to stay out of prison for good

- ❖ Spiritual hierarchy (of your personal choice) this will be your compass that directs your values and molds your character

Add who you like—just make sure that you are not careless in your choosing. The end result may not be to your liking otherwise.

The fact remains that even with the right location and support system, (without the ability to be resilient), you can still fall short of rehabilitation and success.

Recovering readily from whatever life may throw at you is so important. You made it through a conviction, loss of friends and family, even reputation. How? You were resilient; even if you failed to notice that fact.

The time it takes you to bounce back or recover from life isn't as important as the action itself. For some, their conviction was the point of no return. For others, it became a point of reference; a moment in time to always remember and learn from. Which will it be for you?

"Nothing is stronger than the resilience of man except for his unwillingness to be."

Below, list possible location you believe can offer you better opportunities than where you are currently and give a few of those opportunities:

Now list your starting five (supporting cast) and what makes them a part of the team.

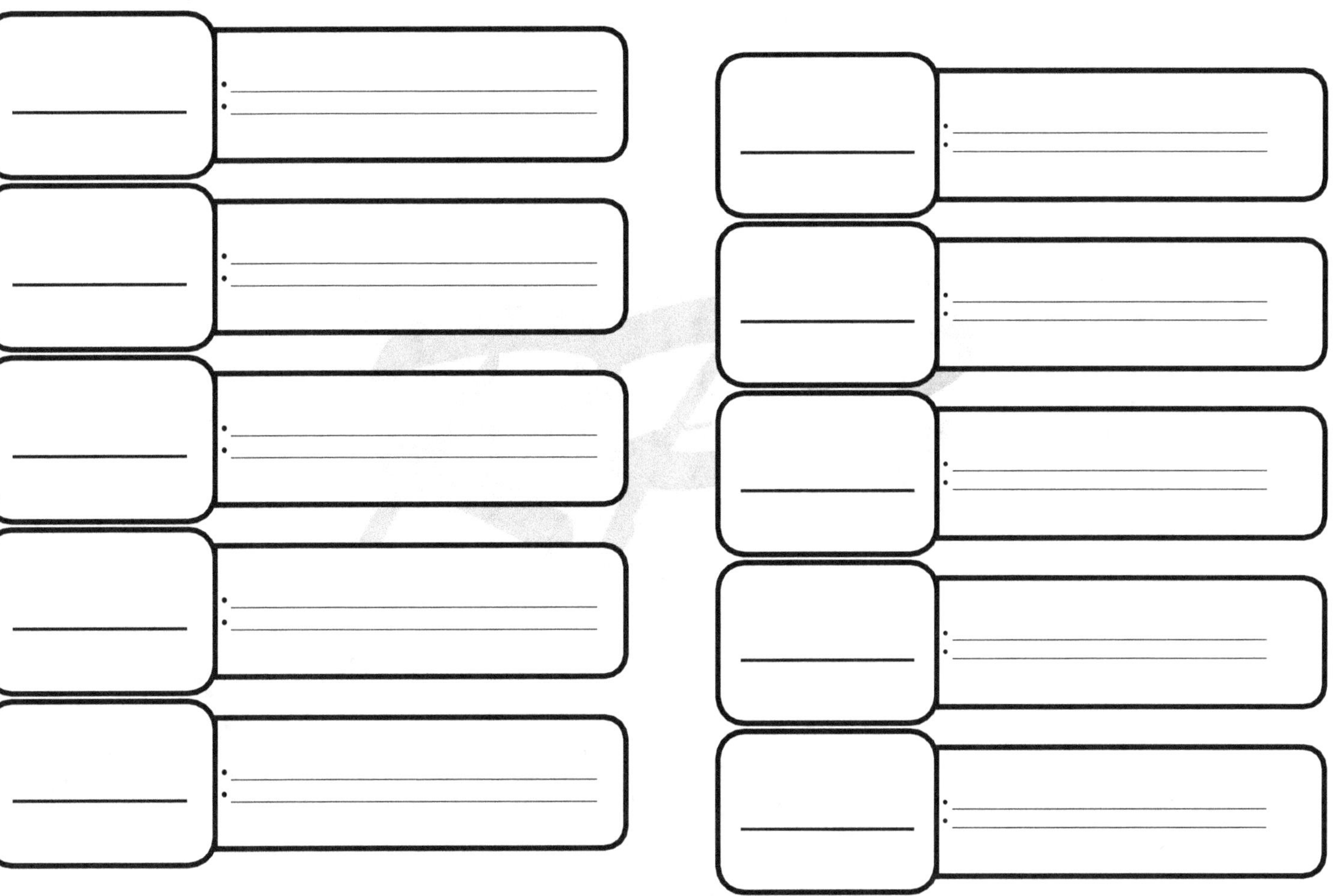

If you list someone that can be removed with the next mistake on their part—don't list them. It makes no sense to hold up a spot for someone who is willing to give it up anyway.

Remember, it is your job to develop your ability to readily recover from whatever may come your way. You will be tested (some more than others), but what you do when you're tested will tell your tale.

G. Sacrificing reputation for character

Is it possible to have a great reputation yet have bad character? What about great character and a bad reputation?

Sounds impossible, right? Well if it sounds like a lie and looks like a lie—than it's probably a lie. Just saying.

"You will become less concerned with what other people think of you when you realize how seldom they do."

-David Wallace

Vocab

Reputation - Notoriety for some particular characteristic; the general estimation that the public has for a person

Character - A characteristic property that defines the apparent individual nature of something; the inherent complex of attributes that determines a person's moral and ethical actions and reactions

Sacrifice - Sell at a loss

What does it mean to sell something at a loss? Well, to me, it means that you are giving up something for something else of lesser value in hope of making a profit of some sort.

We do this with our character (who we are) in hopes that our new found reputation (who we present to others) will bring greater benefits than our now discarded character. What a shame.

This worked for a while before we went to prison. Before we discovered the real value of who we are, but not anymore.

By now, you should have realized that employers hire for character; spouses marry for character; society praises or condemns based on character and the consistency of that character.

A reputation can get you in the door of a great business, in the face of a potential spouse, and in the good graces of a thriving community; however, reputation alone can't extend your stay or presence for very long. You need character.

Don't live your life backwards. Before prison, who people thought we were—motivated us, made us important in many contexts, and it also chauffeured us to prison. It didn't matter to us who we were; how others seen us overshadowed that.

I thought we could care less about what people thought about us? I thought opinions came a dime a dozen. Guess not.

So, now that we are being honest with ourselves, character is what you thought you had. It's what you should desire to revive or—for some—create anew.

"When you have character, opinions matter; when you trade it in for reputation, however, opinions matter too much."

Who you are (at your very core) should define you; not what people say or think. Why? Well the thoughts and opinions of the masses tend to change every day. Who you are—not so much.

Building character takes time. Sometimes more time than you are willing to relinquish. Do it anyway. Following right principles builds character. No other way.

What are right principles? I can't tell you that. It is not my place. The principles that you choose to follow will initially be determined by who you want to be, where you want to go, who you choose to help you along the way, and how you currently want to be remembered by others.

Choose wisely. You have already experienced what life is like living without wisdom and hindsight.

It's time that we stop trying to convince others that we are not going to prison and convince ourselves instead. We suffer the most in the end anyway.

Going forward, when you make big decisions consider which of your attributes will benefit the most: reputation or character. *It's fairly simple after that.*

H. Who can help and who can't (institutional/government resources)

What options do you have now? Who can give you the best assistance for what you are trying to do or struggling with? Will the use of these resources be restricted in any way because you are an ex-felon?

If so, don't panic. There are several entities that were created specifically for you to succeed out in society. They could be nonprofit, state/federal legislature, etc. Don't get caught up on what you can't do when there is so much that you can do.

"Only the truly rehabilitated choose to render to others while being rendered to themselves."

Agency - An administrative unit of government; the state of serving as an official and authorized delegate or agent; how a result is obtained or an end is achieved

Abuse - Change the inherent purpose or function of something; Use wrongly, improperly or excessively;

Request - Express the need or desire for; ask for; Ask (a person) to do something; Inquire for (information)

Requirements - Something that is required in advance

Another part of rehab is engaging the services that are available to you in hopes of ensuring your success in transition and getting the help you need so that you add to your relationships.

This lesson is more informative than anything. We will discuss a few agencies that most of us will need, but there will be several that you can find on your own time during research.

The Department of Alcohol and Other Drug Abuse is a means through which we can access programming to assist our fight against addiction.

If you had a problem using drugs and alcohol before, during, and after prison then you have an addiction that you need to face. It doesn't matter if you feel you can turn it on and off when you need to. Any addiction has the potential to ruin lives; not just yours, so don't play with the beast.

The Department of Employment and Workforce is designed to provide employment benefits, job opportunities, and workforce services that will equip you with the independence that many of us seek through illegal means.

I have witnessed so many come back to prison under the guise of no jobs being available in society. This is just not true. The job you or I may want might not be open but the stepping stones to that job are always open. The goal is to get a job; not the job when you first get out.

Don't set such an impossible standard for yourself. Obtain gainful employment and a creditable work history—then seek for something more to your liking.

Maybe you won't be able to provide the proper medical care for yourself or your children? If so, you can contact *The Department of Health and Human services* which is responsible for providing the distribution of Medicaid benefits.

There is nothing wrong with asking for help with such matters; there is, however, something wrong with not doing so. This agency may help with eye care, hospital visits, physicals for employment, and even dentistry services. All you have to do is apply and follow the rules that come with the services.

For those of you who have children you haven't seen or spouses that restrict you from being a parent to that child/children—you can seek the services of *The Guardian Ad Litem* (through the Department of Administration).

This service is designed to help shine light on the best interest for the child/ children in question. Many times, we struggle to consider how our behavior and incarceration may have affected our children and as a result a Guardian Ad Litem has to get involved to ensure the best results for all parties involved.

Remember that we are in rehab. That we weren't doing things right and so we must be willing to enlist the help of others who are more qualified than ourselves. Before you act, at least ask for their advice. It can make all the difference in the long run.

Another agency that can help with family issues and concerns and the addressing of them is The Department of Social Services. This agency ensures the safety of children and adults who cannot protect themselves and assists families to achieve stability through child support, child care, financial, and other temporary benefits while transitioning into employment.

Why try to do it alone when you don't have to? Why carry a burden that agencies are willing and ready to carry for you until the appropriate time?

Don't have a place to stay or want to acquire better housing? You may want to get some information from *The State Housing Finance and Development Authority*. This service provides assistance to those trying to become first time home owners and those seeking to start out renting a house or apartment.

The information they provide could steer you in a totally different direction than you had already settled on. You may want a house but only make renter's money; you may be making mortgage like payments for rent when you should be buying a house. Request the free information online or in person before you make an ill-advised decision.

Do you struggle with depression or being bi-polar? Do you feel over pressured to make choices that you want more time to consider? Maybe you have failed to properly deal with past trauma and issues that keep impeding your growth as an individual?

In order for you to resurge in society according to plans, you have to consider your level of mental health. *The Department of Mental Health* is designed to support the recovery of individuals with mental illnesses.

Mental illness is defined as any disease of the mind; the psychological state of someone who has emotional or behavioral problems serious enough to require psychiatric intervention.

Don't take your mental health and stability for granted. People who are watching you suffer—are suffering too. They don't know how to help you deal or get better. You may not even want help. Emotional and behavioral instability contributes to suicide, mental/psychotic breaks, and many broken homes and relationships. Take it seriously.

As an ex-offender one of your direct avenues for help is *The Department of Probation, Parole, and Pardon Services* which assists in preparing ex-offenders to become productive citizens in the community.

If you are on parole/probation then you will have an immediate relationship with them due to your reporting and paying fees to stay in society and out of confinement.

You can also check with *PPP* (after meeting requirements) to receive a pardon of past criminal convictions. The requirements may be viewed at their website or through a simple *Google search*. Requirements may vary and it is a case by case basis.

Are you trying to start a business? Don't know exactly what to do or where to start? Then contact *The Small and Minority Business Assistance* (Department of Administration). This agency promotes the growth and development of both small and minority owned businesses in the state of South Carolina. They also advocate so that an equitable portion of state procurement contracts go toward those businesses.

As an ex-offender you may find that you are a minority and can utilize the funds that such an agency can provide to you for the upstart of your venture.

The Department of Vocational Rehabilitation can be beneficial to ex-offenders returning to society. However, the negative is that if you have a drug conviction, they may refuse to service you since you would no longer meet their requirements

They can still provide advice on who may be able to help you get where you are going. Maybe they can direct you to nonprofit organizations that have ready funds to help you prepare for employment and get any needed material that may pertain to that employment.

Before your conviction, did you serve in any branch of the military? If so, there may be benefits that can help you and those you love. *The Office of Veteran's Affairs* will assist you as an ex-service member and your eligible dependents to acquire any benefits that may be open to you all.

This agency may even be able to get you into support groups that can help with your acclimation back into society. As a service member you have seen the best and worst of the world; you have also been the best and worst of society. This is a lot for any one person to deal with—don't deal alone. Get the help you need and find others who understand what you are going through and up against.

Any and all of these services may be provided upon request and the meeting of each agency's requirements. It is your responsibility not to abuse any of the provided services. Doing so could make it harder for others to get such help and services.

When engaging these services be mindful that your path to rehab may intersect with that of others; be sure to network with individuals that may be able to connect you with others who can assist you as well.

I told you rehab was a long process—don't tap out. Keep up the good work and good luck.

I. Accepting responsibility to heal or create relationships

We have done a lot of soul searching as of yet and come to some pretty tough conclusions. *Choices*. You and I decided to commit our crime and unconsciously chose to receive out time of incarceration by default.

It takes a while to come to the conclusion that it was no one's fault but ours. Before that we blamed everyone from the judge to the prison guards because we were incarcerated.

Vocab

Acceptance - A disposition to tolerate or accept people or situations; the mental attitude that something is believable and should be accepted as true

Responsibility - A form of trustworthiness; the trait of being answerable to someone for something or being responsible for one's conduct;

I get that in the beginning it can be hard to accept the fact that you screwed up and have altered the lives of many others besides yourself. However, this point in time must come in order for you to move forward and fix/mend any relationships that will be needed in the future.

These could be any of the following types of relationships:

❖ Parental
❖ Community
❖ Employment
❖ Personal/friendships
❖ Spiritual

Fractures in any of these relationships can lead to dissatisfaction in others.

You can't mend a relationship with your children the same way you would with an employer; different relationship, accountability, expectations, and so on.

It is also true that familial relationships are the hardest ones to fix. Why? It can be many reasons for this: longer duration of relationship, higher potential of let down, and even a trickier road to forgiveness. This is possibly why many ex-offenders don't start in this area.

Starting with this area of relationship says to the other person that you have the time to invest and the attention to see it through. Right out of prison, however, we normally don't and instead of making that clear in the onset, we promise to get to it— though we rarely do.

Count the cost of relationship. If a relationship needs to be mended, don't start mending if you can't spare the energy, time, and resources to perform it. Every time you promise to and don't, you are creating a greater rift in that relationship. Do this too much and there won't be a relationship to mend.

Hence why priorities are so important when dealing with rehab. Straight out of prison your first goal is to what? Find employment, build another financial foundation for yourself, and/or probation, parole, or community supervision fees; not mending relationships.

When telling this to someone it may sound selfish and inconsiderate but it is only the truth. You may get all types off reactions simply because they're not used to hearing the truth from you. The reality of selflessness and consideration is: truth.

Family and friends may be aloof for a while. Don't panic. The community may be skeptical of you for their own reasons—don't worry about it. Jobs may tell you no more often than not—it's ok. There are plenty of other jobs out there to apply for.

Your main job—fresh out of prison—is to stay focused on your end game. Keep seeking the compensation of all your hard work and rehab. It will come.

Now your spiritual relationship is bigger and different than the rest of your relationships. Your higher power will determine how you view and engage your broken relationships. This becomes your true north. Something resides in this area of your being—whether you want to admit it or not. Use it for your betterment; not your detriment.

Familial- Admit that you can't chang the past, but are committed to doing better i the future. Encourage them to allow things to happen natually so that you are not held to time restrictions.

Employment- Be honest. Admit that you may not be the best option for the job, but that you have more to lose than those whc are more qualified. Ensure them that you won't take it for granted.

Community- They normally don't know too much about you apart fro the news or gossip; show them by example; not word play. They will buy-in to you when and if you buy-i to yourself. Remember that.

Spiritual- For this to matter, you have to choose for yourself. Don't follow just because you admire others. Know why y believe what you believe. If you are inconsistent in this area so will you be in the rest of your life.

Doing the things in this lesson will help you when you have to create relationships anew. Once you know your limits and what your faults/tendencies are, you will be able to better present yourself to others. They will be able to take you or leave you—having all the facts of who you are and what they may gain by being in relationship with you.

You want a good test about relationship:
look at what you know about yourself, what
damage you are responsible for, what
measure have you put in place to heal and
diminish that damage, who have you
become now?

Would you be in relationship with you?
Going through this will help you deal more
with the responses of those you love and
those you may seek relationship with.

*"You can't expect people to
respect a person if you don't;
particularly if that person is
you."*

J. Finding the balance of consistency

Have you ever had tunnel vision? Been too focused in one area of your life so much that the others suffer? This can happen when you are rehabbing yourself.

Don't overdo it. Every area is important but all areas can't be urgent. It would also behoove you to understand that most times when you operate in one area—it alters another (either for good/bad).

Vocab

Multi-focus – the ability to concentrate one's attention or give special emphasis to more than one object or area

Balance - Equality of distribution; harmonious arrangement or relation of parts or elements within a whole

Tunnel vision - Visual impairment involving a loss of peripheral vision

Dimensional atrophy – weakening or deprivation of one's attribution dimensions due to lack of use or over use in one area over the others

Like we discussed in the last lesson, your mind will be on one area in particular when you get out, but it doesn't excuse us from activity or influence in other areas.

What is in your peripheral: family, a place to stay, counseling, spiritual awakening, outreach? If you look long and hard you will see the connection between each area that is important to you.

For instance, employment affects every area of your being. Too much of it kidnaps your attention from any other area; too little of it restricts potential impact on those same areas. No one ever said rehab was going to be easy.

Not being aware of these effects/changes within dimensions can cause something I call dimensional atrophy.

Lack of balance can kill or destroy. Too much water in the kitchen sink; too much carbon dioxide and not enough oxygen; too much imagination and not enough reality— the list is vast. However, the principle is clear: too much to one—deprives from another; both overuse and the lack thereof can cause atrophy.

We have to develop the ability to concentrate our attention on different dimensions both equally and simultaneously.

Making a living shouldn't take away from you being a good father or a better husband. Becoming a better man shouldn't make you a worse citizen. Seeking a higher power shouldn't reduce your inner power. Balance is king.

In the following exercise write your dimensions of focus and how they interact.

List also how you can positively influence one while you are in another.

Dimension:

Description:

Description:

Description:

Dimension:

Description:

Description:

Description:

Dimension:

Description:

Description:

Description:

Dimension:

Description:

Description:

Description:

Use the information that you have written down to better adapt to the many relationships and their demands going forward.

Remember this won't happen overnight. So be willing to put forth the effort and see it through to the end. Good luck.

Level 3 defined: Exhibiting no abrupt variations; steady. Rational and balanced; sensible

Dimensional application: Working out the kinks of rehab and becoming rational and balanced in everyday lawful living.

Dimension: Realignment of the offender to society

Points of focus:

A. Introducing yourself to the community

What does it mean to put your best foot forward? How do you broadcast your strengths without minimizing your weaknesses? How much of yourself needs to be seen by the community anyway? How much should you even care about their opinion?

Vocab

Stimulus - Make someone or something act in a particular way or do a particular thing; excite the feelings or emotions of; disturb the peace of; provide the needed stimulus for

Compensation - a defense mechanism that conceals your undesirable shortcomings by exaggerating desirable behaviors

Rapport - A relationship of mutual understanding or trust and agreement between people

Continuity - Uninterrupted connection or union

If you haven't already figured out from the definitions—you're the stimulus. By living out your new life day to day you will incite in others a willingness to be intrigued with your odd behavior.

Why odd? This version of you is totally different to your community. You were someone different when you left; the assumption will be that you will be the same when you return.

However, since you are not the same—they have to meet you again. Get to know you anew. Who says you only get one time to make an impression?

Be mindful that something else has also taken place in your community: disturbance of peace. The world as they knew it (during your absence) has been altered. Not everyone in your community will be disturbed to have you back; some have been waiting for this day all along.

Your personal neighborhood is comprised of those who've seen your short comings and the few that have seen your potential. Start with the potential clairvoyants.

By starting with them, you are starting with level ground. You are less likely to get demonized when you mess up fresh out of prison. Even though these few members of the community hold personal expectations for you—they won't disrupt the progress they foresee.

The naysayers should be the least of your worries. You may not have sway with them right now but soon you will. Just be consistent in what you do. Those who fail to buy-in from firsthand encounters may very well be won over by the eager to be applauded clairvoyants.

As your rapport with the community begins to grow don't get sidetracked. They are not enamored with what they have been showed; they are simply intrigued enough to see what happens next. This means that any failure on your part to compensate for your weaknesses may result in a hit in the continuity department.

Without building this continuity/connection with the neighborhood you forsake a potential support system. These members of a much bigger society—know people and can help pave the way for your immediate success/future victories. Don't underestimate the power of people and their opinions; whether you agree with them or not.

"The pathway to success is beaten by the many who seek to pave a clearer way for the few."

What to do?

- ✓ **Don't go above and beyond** in anything unless you are willing to do so in everything. Refrain from raising the bar of expectation too high—too

quickly. Doing so will not always end well.

- ✓ **Actually introduce yourself** to neighbors you may not know in the community. Don't assume they don't like you if they don't know you.
- ✓ **Offer help and assistance** only when doing so has a moderate to least chance of misinterpretation. Meaning well won't always go over well with your peers.
- ✓ **Get out and about sometimes**. Let the community see you in the context of community. Take a walk; take a run; heck, take a walk after you run—just let people see what you're like when the pressure is off and you're just living life. This will be the ideal time to spend time with the children. When people see that you're living for someone other than yourself their hearts may soften all the more.
- ✓ **Welcome advice** from different members of your community from time to time. People tend to care more about the end result when they feel as if they have contributed to the immediate process. Valuing tends to go both ways you know.
- ✓ **Act how you desire others to act.** The new you doesn't want to be judged beforehand; don't do it to others either. It's simple: if you don't know, don't assume.

B. Keep it 100; speak for yourself

Don't you hate it when someone speaks up in your steed before you have the chance to speak for yourself? Or have you ever felt weird because another person has to defend you because you haven't put yourself in the position to defend yourself?

You know what you did to go to prison. You know what you are doing to keep from going back. When it matters, speak up for yourself. I promise you that for every issue you fail to answer for—someone else will. At least yours will be true.

Vocab

Transparency - The quality of being clear and transparent

Consider - Judge or regard; look upon; regard or treat with consideration, respect, and esteem

Credibility - The quality of being believable or trustworthy

At stake - In question or at issue; to be won or lost; at risk

Attest - Provide evidence for; stand as proof of; show by one's behavior, attitude, or external attributes; authenticate, affirm to be true, genuine, or correct, as in an official capacity;

Excel - Distinguish oneself

Tendency - A characteristic likelihood of or natural disposition toward a certain condition or character or effect; an attitude of mind especially one that favors one alternative over others

News flash: You don't get automatic credibility just because you maxed out your sentence; you do, however, gain the suspicions of everyone around you. So, would you want people who are suspicious of you speaking up for you? Don't answer that.

Your actions and word play should attest to the individual you have become. Now sometimes actions and words can be misinterpreted, but if you stay consistent—even that will work itself out or eliminate the interpreter altogether.

How do you gain credibility?

1. *Give your word and keep it*
2. *Do all things as if you stand to lose everything*
3. *Admit when you're wrong*
4. *Consistently become better; never settle*

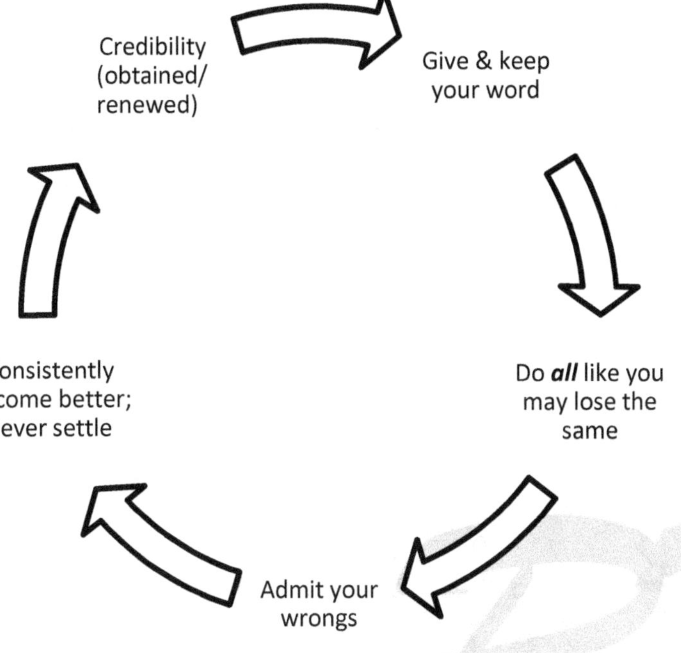

The more you realize what is at stake in your transition the more others will focus on what you stand to gain. The things that you stand to lose are:

- Freedom
- Good rapport
- Community/family support
- Opportunity
- Credibility
- Legacy
- Influence

How you transition will either secure these for you or make it impossible for you to obtain them. No other options. Keep this mindset and you will be fine; take it for granted and reap what you sow.

"The proactive approach to a mistake is to acknowledge it instantly, correct and learn from it. This literally turns a failure into a success."

--*Stephen Covey*

Once you gain credibility you will find it easier to be transparent with people in almost any situation. Why? Because you have uprooted the things you were ashamed of, replaced manipulation with character, and transformed from felon to ex-offender.

People will start to consider you as an individual; not a criminal. They will sit back and observe your body of work as evidence of your change; not your guilt. They will begin to respect you for who you have become; regardless of where you've come from. They will make an effort to esteem you because through your rehabilitation you have esteemed yourself. Wow.

C. Find ways to repay your debt

One of the best ways to get yourself away from the past is to make amends for it. Nothing screams penitence louder than community service and mentoring, especially in the sphere of your criminal history.

What took you to prison? How did it impact your life? How do you think it will affect the lives of others in similar situations? Do you believe that your experience can encourage other people not to make the same mistakes?

In order for your contributions to make the greatest impact abroad you have to start at home. The individuals in your community know you best of all—especially if you are sticking to the plan. So, they will be able to direct you to those who may be susceptible to a life of crime. Who knows you...may be the deciding factor.

Vocab

Influence - The effect of one thing (or person) on another; A power to affect persons or events especially power based on prestige etc.

Impressionable - Easily impressed or influenced

Germaneness - Pertinence by virtue of a close relation to the matter at hand

Probability - A measure of how likely it is that some event will occur; a number expressing the ratio of favorable cases to the whole number of cases possible; The quality of being probable; a probable event or the most probable event

Role model - Someone worthy of imitation

Veracity - The quality of being truthful; The quality of being correct, true, or close to the true value; Unwillingness to tell lies

Have you noticed anyone in your community who reminds you of you? If not, they are there—you just have to take time to observe. If you had someone speaking in your ears the truth of where you were headed maybe you could have avoided prison altogether; some of you did have those potent whispers, yet through your living—you made criminal conviction inevitable.

Surely, we don't want that for anyone else now do we? Your situation is unique; not that others haven't been to prison—they have—but what you learned there and how it affected you is tied to your personal story. What could it do for others?

Grab one; grab a few, just grab someone headed down the wrong road and tell them your story. Express the impact it had on your loved ones. Paint a truthful picture of what prison is like and dispel all the nonsense portrayed by TV and music. Stop their silly dreaming before it becomes a nightmare.

Doing so will give them an opportunity to recognize the veracity of your testimony and give credence to the germaneness of your journey back home. Majority of the time, if you tell the truth, these individuals are impressionable enough that you can sway them away from their harmful behavior.

Make sure, however, that you do not force them to take your word for it. Simply give your story and relate to them the probability of prison time if they continue down the road to destruction.

"History only repeats itself when those living in the present forget about it or downplay its relevance on their future."

Whether you like it or not you are a role model to someone—good or bad. You don't get to choose who watches you—who observes your actions, or what perception they take away from that moment. The most impactful choice of action you have in life is to be intentional in everything you do.

I am not suggesting that you do anything new at this level. You have always been intentional: when you lived a life of crime—you were intentional; why not be intentional while influencing others to be better? Never underestimate the power of influence. It has the ability to change lives.

Period of criminal behavior	Conviction for criminal behavior	Payment of debt
Lawless living Lack of empathy Inaccurate self-view Inaccurate pardigm Lack of awareness/ No concern for consequences	Result of behavior Check from reality Awareness of effects on others Willingness to address those effects for self/others	Sowing seeds of rehabilitation in community Mentoring youth and wayward individuals Living the example of change Becoming a conduit of change

I was always taught that the hard part is getting through the bidding process; not really. The hardest part, to me, is reentering society and making amends for past mistakes.

Why? Because if you didn't put in the work during the bid then you won't get the results in society. It's that simple. It is in society that you first begin to pay your debt to others; your time in prison, however, is considered payment to yourself.

You have to take care of self before you intentionally invest in others. Just like in business:

1. Trust and believe in your self-investment
2. Put in the work towards your goals
3. Gain the trust and belief of others around you

Self then others. There is no other way to achieve successful reintegration without inward and outward investments.

When you buy-in to yourself others will buy-in to you and by default your vision for healthy reintegration.

"Societal debt has the ability to be either an inspiring stimulus or a crippling liability."

As always, payment—sincere payment- is your choice; not an obligation by any means.

D. Educate yourself about any restrictions you have as an offender

What restrictions are hindering you now that you are out of prison? Which restrictions are temporary/permanent? How does this affect your overall game plan?

Being an ex-offender brings with it many restrictions that tend to hit us in the face at every turn. Being unprepared or unwilling to deal with them could spell disaster for a successful transition.

Vocab

Limitation - A principle that limits the extent of something; an act of limiting or restricting (as by regulation)

Allowances - A permissible difference; allowing some freedom to move within limits

Leverage - Strategic advantage; power to act effectively

Investigate - Conduct an inquiry or investigation of

For some of us community supervision is a reality and with that comes certain limitations:

- ✓ Ankle monitors
- ✓ Supervision fees
- ✓ Curfews
- ✓ Check in dates
- ✓ Consequences for completion failure

The list gets long and redundant and a majority of the requirements are tied into the consequences. Knowing your limitations should be first on your list of transition since failure in this area could revoke any further opportunities of uninterrupted freedom.

Once you know what you can't do—become aware of what you can do. Restrictions are only limiting to those who refuse to find a way in spite of them.

There are no absolutes; for every restriction there is an allowance that lessens the restraining force. With community supervision you have to be home at a certain time. However, you are not restricted in how that time is used (within reason).

Through investigation you can determine what's a go and what's a no. Once you know, be sure to tell all relevant parties: employers, family, and other supporting cast. This prevents any violations being presented by those depending on you for results.

Like restrictions, allowances may have time constraints. What may be allowed within the first few weeks may not be allowed at later times; contra wise, what isn't allowed out the gate may be allowed later on.

Be sure to ask those in the position to give you firm answers. Remember, a mistake in this area may be viewed as a deliberate defiance of established restrictions.

When investigating, don't be afraid to ask questions. Who cares if they've been asked before? Who cares if no one else has ever asked that question? This is your freedom; leave nothing to chance.

"I have learned that when one's mind is made up, fear diminishes; knowing what must be done does away with fear."

- Rosa Parks

Now what is the game of life without a little leverage? Other allowances can only be accessed through your use of leverage. Now I am not referring to you putting the *tim-down* on others. I am only suggesting that if you have used your time wisely in prison there may be more options open to you.

For instance, if you gained a GED while in prison you have more options than those who did not. If you gained communication skills, OJT's, networked with volunteers, engaged available reentry programs, then you have options: leverage.

In the space provided below list some of the things you have gained that can be used as leverage:

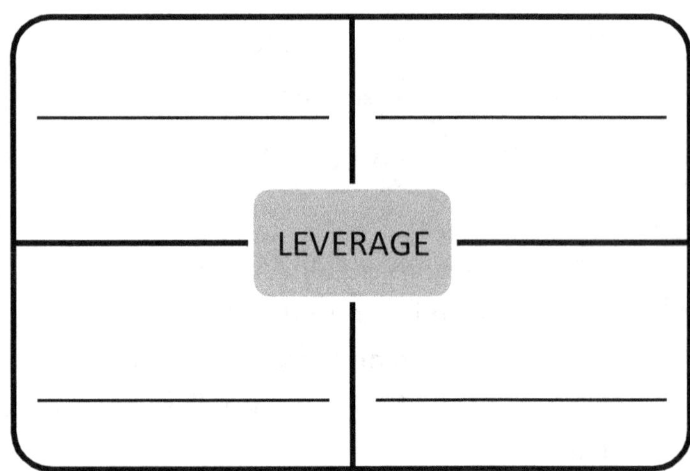

How you use your leverage is key. Don't use it in areas where doing so would minimize your character or self-worth, nor that of others. There is nothing wrong with doing the hard work—even when you feel you don't have to—if you know that work will lead to better results and needed experience.

"Failure to take one's incarceration and it's opportunities in stride will inevitably bring one's future to a halt."

E. Refuse to doubt your ability to succeed

"No matter how many supporters exist to spur you on your way, progress won't result if you have neither the will nor the faith to step out."

Is it possible to convince others to believe in you if you are failing to convince yourself? Do you need the faith of others initially or can you first step out in faith?

We desire to be first in many things, however, when it comes to change our hands are down and our lips are sealed. We want to see someone else succeed; we need examples. But what if we were to be the example?

Vocab

Initiative - Readiness to embark on bold new ventures;

Disadvantage - The quality of having an inferior or less favorable position; a flaw or weak point

Doubt - The state of being unsure of something; Uncertainty about the truth, factuality or existence of something

Will - A fixed and persistent intent or purpose

Example - A task performed or problem solved in order to develop skill or understanding; something/someone to be imitated

Progress - Gradual improvement, growth or development; the act of moving forward (as toward a goal)

Why should you doubt yourself? Trust me there are enough doubters to go around—they don't need you. When you doubt yourself or your abilities to make it on the outside you put yourself at a disadvantage.

No matter the amount of work that you have put in during your incarceration and period of release—without faith of success—you won't survive when the naysayers arise.

You are not doing it for them; you are doing it for you first. So, it should be the same when it comes to your ability to succeed. As long as you believe that you can—you can.

Now I'm not saying that you won't have moments of doubt every now and again; on the contrary, I'm just saying that it should remain momentary. Your will has to be stronger than your longest moment of doubt.

There has to be in your mind's eye a picture of you achieving your desired goals. When in doubt you must persist. Successful transition into society should be your purpose and intent every day you wake up.

"People don't have faith in dreams; they have faith in a

person's ability to bring a dream into reality."

When you overcome self-doubt, you will be ready to exercise the initiative needed to become an example for others. Many will see you achieving goals that others said were unattainable and unrealistic. At the same time, you will be developing both skill and understanding that many will learn from and imitate.

If you continue in this path you will gain something that people will fail to notice at first: progress. They won't notice it because progress isn't some grand thing with flashing lights screaming look at me. No, it's a hindsight view of several choices, mistakes, rebounds, and victories that depict gradual improvement in areas of difficulty, maturity as an individual, and stability in action.

Notice the word: mistakes. A mistake is nothing more than a warning sign that promotes continual effort with something or someone. You will have many of them—don't count. They are never meant to limit you; they are meant to strengthen or condition you to be better. Value them.

How do you know when you are making progress and not just spinning your wheels? Compare where you are with where you're trying to go. In the space provided describe what success is and the first five steps you need to take in order the reach the latter ones:

Definition of success:

____
____
____
____
____
____
____
____
_______________.

Step one:

____
____
____
____
____
____
____
________________________.

Step two:

____
____
____
____
____
____
________________________.

Step three:

____
____
____

____
____
____
____
____
_______________________________________.

Step four:

____
____
____
____
____
____
____
_______________________________________.

Step five:

____
____
____
____
____
____
____
_______________________________________.

Use these steps as a gauge to see whether or not you are making progress during transition. If you find yourself becoming stagnant or going backwards re-examine your steps. Refrain from changing your definition of success; modify how you achieve it all you want. Good luck.

"The only true security in life comes from knowing that every single day you are improving yourself in some way…increasing the caliber of who you are…if every day you constantly improve your ability to enjoy your life, then you'll experience it at a level of richness most people never even dream of."

--Anthony Robbins

(See *Extras* section page for another exercise)

F. Respect the opinions of others

When it comes to engaging a successful transition into society, the opinions of others hold influence.

Does it mean that their opinions are right—not necessarily. It does however mean that they can prompt consideration in the minds of those who matter to your transition.

"Most men are incapable of expressing opinions that differ much from the prejudices of their social upbringing."

-Einstein

Vocab

Forethought - Planning or plotting in advance of acting; Judiciousness in avoiding harm or danger

Persuasive - Intended or having the power to induce action or belief

Appease - Cause to be more favorably inclined; gain the good will of; overcome or allay; Make peace with

Consider this: during your incarceration you were foolish to say the least. Disrespectful when you didn't get your way. Intolerable when you were forced to comply with institutional rules. These are smoke signals.

What if your new potential employer happens to be a close family member of a warden, officer, or staff member who knows you? What do you think will be said when your name comes up?

Or what if the victims of your case don't feel that you have paid your debt of punishment yet? And they choose to call every employer you get and advise them of your misdeeds. True or not, would this not become a burden on your place of employment? The power of opinions.

So, what do you do?

Plan in advance for the potential influence or sway that anyone may have upon your transition. Who have you offended? How did you offend them and can it be mended with a little effort?

Whether you like it or not as an ex-offender you will have to appease the unreasonable—within reason. Because of the damage caused by your crime there will also be some damage made in the repairing process.

Have you ever witnessed a rock slide (in person/on the news)? Dirt and rocks break away from their foundation due to heavy rain and conditions. They normally impact the public in one way or another. Once the damage is done and it's time for cleanup, work crews cause minimal damage to both the unstable foundation and whichever landscape the slide now covers.

So it is with transitioning. Your *criminal land slide* inconvenienced several people, some of which you have no knowledge of. Nevertheless, in order for repair to be effective and not just cosmetic—you will incur some damage from public opinion.

The damage you will incur is nothing compared to the success you stand to gain if you incur it willingly.

If you can't get in contact with someone who may have bearing on a potential employer before you apply for a job—be brutally honest about yourself during the interview. Let them know that you haven't always done the right things in life or by other people, but that you are committed to doing better. Ensure them that the consideration of being employed at their business is a step in the right direction.

At the end of the day remember this:

"Your determination to succeed and the opinions of others have one thing in common…the ability to persuade others."

Since everyone is entitled to their opinion, the only thing we can do on a consistent basis is respect it. Respect is not agreement. You are simply affirming another's right to speak their mind and be heard.

This lesson is very crucial. Every relationship that you will ever engage can and may very well be influenced by the opinion of another person.

Use what you know about yourself and those with whom you interact to properly judge those opinions.

G. Build bridges not barriers

"Barriers have always been bridges; the real question is which do you see?"

Being a convicted felon, being absent from the lives of your children, no car to get to work, no ready money to get started, the community being against you, etc.

How do you see these? Barriers that would take too much energy to get past or bridges of uncharted territory that have the potential to produce powerful experiences and results?

Vocab

Bad blood - A feeling of ill will arousing active hostility

Barrier - A structure or object that impedes free movement; any condition that makes it difficult to make progress or to achieve an objective; anything serving to maintain separation by obstructing vision or access

Bridge - A structure that allows people…to cross an obstacle…

Resolve - Understand the meaning of; Reach a decision; Reach a conclusion after a discussion or deliberation; Bring to an end; come to a final conclusion

Perception - A way of regarding situations or topics etc. The appearance of things relative to one another as determined by their distance from the viewer

Usage - Accepted or habitual practice; the amount or manner in which something is used or consumed

Most barriers can be crossed and left in the past if you only change both:

> ➢ How you perceive them
> ➢ How you use them

For example, what is the purpose of a fence? Is it to keep things/people in or is it to keep them out? This is defined by whoever puts the fence up in the first place.

Bad blood between people (such as family, friends, employers, and the community) can be mutual. However, when it comes to institutions (such as state laws/restrictions/consequences) it is only personal. How is that?

People can attach meaning; institutions cannot. So bad blood towards an institution will remain a barrier until you decide to resolve your feelings and attach new meaning to the institution in question.

The burden is solely upon you. Change how you operate within the confines of such institutions and by so doing, eliminate bad blood.

Now because of the potential of two meanings existing at the same time, in regards to people, simply changing how you feel and attaching new meaning won't be so easy.

In relationships of all types you are a co-owner of the particular barrier. You can forgive, move on, and even put a construction sign on your end; you can't force others to retaliate in kind.

Why build half a bridge? Turning your end into a bridge leaves open the opportunity for the other person to begin construction and meet you in the middle of a completed bridge.

It also allows you to remove a barrier that consumes needed energy to keep it in place. Once you forgive, ask forgiveness, do the work, and refocus your energies, you are free to build other bridges elsewhere.

A failure to reconstruct barriers into bridges is an admittance that people, institutions, and circumstances can and will continue to determine your direction in life and level of success. This in and of itself is a barrier.

To focus on rehabilitation and successful transition—you need bridges. You need avenues that when accessed can contribute to your efforts.

If you have been applying the lessons in the previous levels, then you are in a perfect position to start building.

Components of bridges and opportunities:

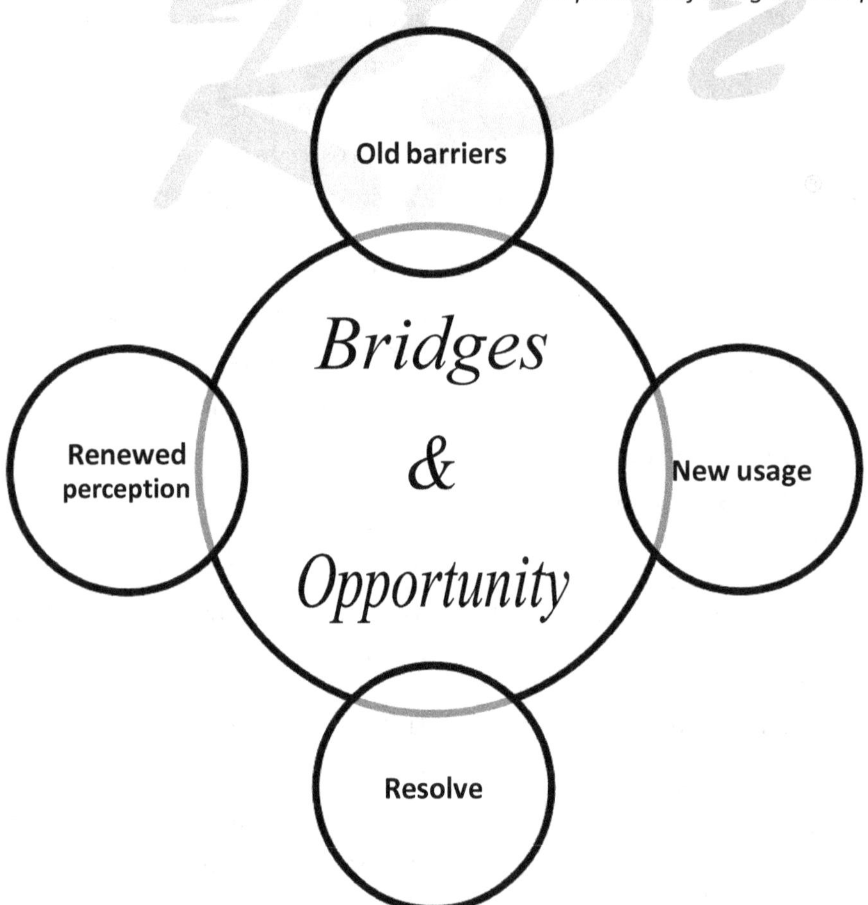

H. Be intentional
   ## (words and actions)

What does it mean to be intentional? Is it not making mistakes? Is it making mistakes and taking responsibility for them? Is it doing something on purpose or is it doing something with a purpose?

Vocab

Intentional - Characterized by conscious design or purpose; done, made or performed with purpose and intent

Purpose - An anticipated outcome that is intended or that guides your planned actions; the quality of being determined to do or achieve something;
firmness of purpose

Timid - Lacking conviction, boldness or courage

Careless - Marked by lack of attention, consideration, forethought or thoroughness; not careful; effortless and unstudied

Flounder - Walk with great difficulty; behave awkwardly; have difficulties

Haphazard - Dependent upon or characterized by chance; marked by great carelessness

"Man has the unreasonable desire to be judged not by what they've done, but by what they meant to do."

Before we chose to change our lives, we lived out the aforementioned quote every day. We went to jail but didn't mean to get caught. We abandoned our family yet didn't intend for anyone to get hurt.

Your word only holds weight if it is backed by thought infused action. Being intentional means that you have considered the actions, their consequences, and their effects on the lives of others—before you take them.

All the work that you have put forth by completing all the lessons up to this point has defined your purpose. Every day you should be anticipating the fruition of your hard work—if not why do it? The lessons have become a blueprint for your success; an impetus if you will.

Every action that you take during your transition should be marked by a high degree of conviction. Timidity has no place in your efforts. Sure you can be cautious about making certain decisions that have the potential of great risk; but not timid.

Being timid in your efforts is like enacting your plans for success with little to no faith that you will achieve them—this can't happen.

Were you timid when you were committing your crimes? Did you lack the confidence that you would get away with it? Probably not; you believed you were good until you weren't. *Facts.*

You were careless, not paying attention to how you were moving; living for the present with no thought for the future. Not now; you can't afford to flounder at this junction in your life.

Are you reading this material because you were forced to or because you desired to? This is the difference between being haphazard and being intentional.

Your goal is to be intentional in all your actions while leaving room for the occasional moments of chance and circumstance. Chance is not a guarantee; don't go through your transition period dependent on it. Have a plan and implement it.

People normally refuse to take responsibility for the things/actions that we didn't intend to happen. However, when we have put forth a plan and carried it out, we are in a position where we can explain our intentions and apologize for the results. This is your goal.

"If you fail to consider the action, you have forfeited your right to complain about the outcome."

Intentional action = **desired purpose of events**

I. Don't forget the history

One thing that each individual has in surplus is history. We have so much of it that we can't review it all in one lifetime.

History is individual and collective in nature. We can learn from our history and those of others—if we so choose to. However, we should never forget it.

Vocab

Forget - Dismiss from the mind; stop remembering;

Individual - Being or characteristic of one particular part of many; separate and distinct from others of the same kind; characteristic of or meant for a single person or thing; concerning one person exclusively

Collective - Done by or characteristic of individuals acting together

History - The continuum of events occurring in succession leading from the past to the present and even into the future; All that is remembered of the past as preserved in writing; a body of knowledge

"He who causes history to reoccur is in a state of stupidity; not déjà vu."

Your past can become your wheel of success or the spoke if you will of each and every one of your endeavors.

Our histories are viewed in positive or negative light depending on the context we surround them with. If you have a *bad history,* is it not because you have failed to bring the good out of it? Contra wise, many who have *good histories* have found a way to make lemonade from lemons.

You may find that several lessons overlap by the mention of the past. This is not a typo but an intentional act. Out of the three: past, present, and future, it is the past that holds the most bearing upon our life.

The past can dictate our present circumstances and shape our future outcomes. Bewildering isn't it?

So, as it stands you have a written history called a record. A record that is public information for anyone who may be wondering who you are or why you act the way you do. This is the body of knowledge for those who don't know enough about you.

"What others see in the present is the point of reference by which they view your past mistakes."

I say that history is both individual and collective because your individual history can be interrupted and molded by the histories of those you surround yourself with.

In South Carolina the law states: *...hands of one is the hands of all*. If you are with others in the commission of a crime you are just as guilty—even if you turn state's evidence or escape criminal prosecution.

In society it is pretty much the same. You will be judged according to actions not context of circumstance. You are still on the continuum of life from which there is no jumping of the tracks.

It is because of these facts that people like you and I willingly choose to dismiss their history from their minds. *It didn't happen. That wasn't me. I don't really remember.* We don't have to do this anymore. Instead of hitting the stop button on your memory systems, look and see what you can learn from it. There just may be a diamond in the ruff after all.

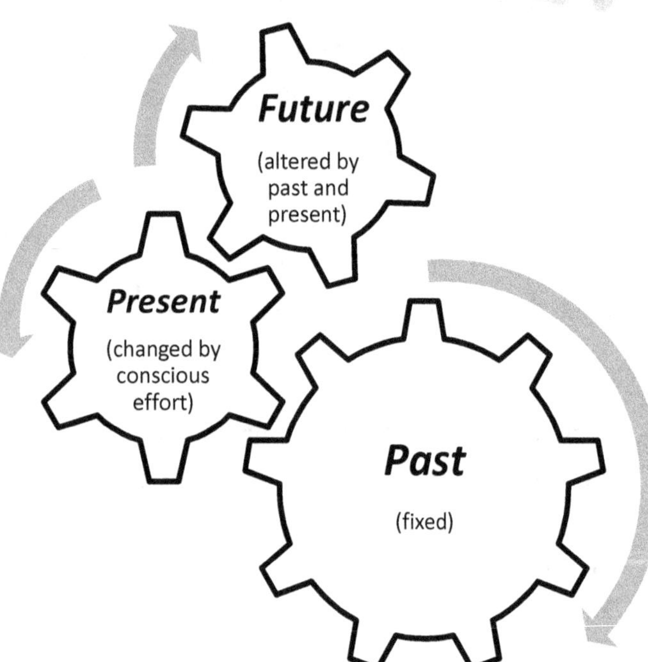

Every day you are redefining and shaping your past and future. Looking at the wheel, you see that as one turns—so turns the others. **Live in this reality.** Consider the following:

- Your *past* can't be changed; it is fixed in terms of time. However, how it is viewed is ever-changing.
- Your *present* can be changed with every conscious effort you employ in the moment. Your conscious effort can be both hindered by the influence of your past and what you desire for the future.
- Your *future* is also ever-changing. Since it has yet to be, the influence of the past and the efforts of the present continually alter what it is to become.

Dismissing your past and choosing to live in the moment (only) will be more detrimental to you and your future than to the collective whole. History deserves your attention; don't cheat yourself on this one. Try this helpful process:

1. *Stop*
2. *Reflect*
3. *Discern changes*
4. *Determine present and future effects*
5. *Apply*
6. *Repeat*

It may be worth noting that some of us have histories that we have blocked away for numerous reasons. No matter how painful your past may be, the only way for you to live fully in your present and succeed in your future is to deal with it mentally, emotionally, and physically in reality.

Look at it this way the pain and ignorance of your past can only hinder you if you leave it as is. You are different now than you were then. Learn, grow, and build beyond your past.

Level 4 defined: A natural or proper position, place or stage. Being of the same degree of rank, standing, or advantage as another; equal.

Dimensional application: Rising again to the level of citizenship enjoyed by your peers in society.

Dimension: Reclaiming one's citizenship and standing

Points of focus:

A. Revaluing what you took for granted

By now you should see everything in a new light. Things should mean more—appraised at a higher value. The new you should have a new view.

Can you say that this is true about you yet? You have obtained most of what you lost and have all the opportunity in front of you to go beyond that. The power of progress.

Vocab

Estimate - The classification of someone or something with respect to its worth; an expert estimation of the quality, quantity, and other characteristics of someone or something

Hindsight - Understanding the nature of an event after it has happened

Addition - A component that is added to something to improve it; something added to what you already have;

Summation - the process whereby multiple stimuli can produce a response…that one stimulus alone does not produce

Mutualism - The relation between two different species of organisms that are interdependent; each gains benefits from the other

See before we pretended that we valued family at let's say a 10; when in reality, we valued them at a 5. No, this isn't true for you? Why did you go to prison and leave them?

If you lived a life of crime—no matter what it was, you did not value your family, your freedom, your faith, or your rights *the way you should have.*

As they say, *the understanding of an event after it has happened (hindsight) is 20/20.* However, that is only if you are looking in its direction.

"One cannot be taught unless he first seeks to learn; if any seeks to be taught—they must also be willing."

A friend of mine (*Todd Bussey*) always taught that we are one or two things after incarceration:

1. An **addition** (having revalued our position in life, family, society, etc. and living in accordance with that new estimation)
2. A **subtraction** (continuing to undervalue those we love and the circumstances that surround them)

Which are you? Which do you want to be? Again, it's your choice.

In the spaces provide below list five areas/people you undervalued before incarceration; then list five areas/people that you have reappraised since your release and placed them at their proper position in your life:

Undervalued

1.__________________________________

2.__________________________________

3.__________________________________

4.__________________________________

5.__________________________________

Reappraised

1.__________________________________

2.__________________________________

3.__________________________________

4.__________________________________

5.__________________________________

Your list may be exactly the same for both or it may have a few variations. Why? Well some undervalued relationships may have ceased to exist altogether or may be even less important to you at this stage in your life.

It could also be that you overvalued some relationships before prison that you had to put back in their proper place. Whatever the case, your actions should begin to line up with reappraisal that the new rehabbed version of you agrees with.

"Peace of mind comes when you realize that you can regain most of what you once lost and that what's left behind wasn't worth retaining anyway."

B. Continuing education
(self-help and more)

Now that you know what you want to do in life, how will you further your knowledge and experience in that area to increase both enjoyment and income? Education. There isn't much that you can do without a decent degree of continued education.

Don't panic! You don't have to go to school for umpteen years for it to classify as education; don't rule out the possibility though. No, you can get certified in several different areas of expertise and gain both knowledge and experience in the process.

Vocab

Certification - Confirmation that some fact or statement is true through the use of documentary evidence; validating the authenticity of something or someone

Experience - The accumulation of knowledge or skill that results from direct participation in events or activities; be subject to, have the experience of

Intern - A student who works (often without pay) in order to gain experience

Novel - Original and of a kind not seen before; pleasantly new or different

Self-worth - The quality of being worthy of esteem or respect

Continuing your education can increase the percentage of success for each individual who chooses to engage the process.

Alright, so when we look at our society today, we notice that many people have degrees and no job. Is this because of the degree or the individual?

It could be both. Sometimes the school in which we obtain the degree may not be as recognized as others (for your field). Or you may pursue a career initially and change your mind by graduation; then you go back for something else. What a waste, right?

Degrees are not your only options. Others, who tire of the agony of obtaining degrees, strive to get certifications instead. Certifications, like degrees, have the ability to boost your potential earning capacity and put you in a better position to support your current and future ambitions.

The truth is people make the mistake of getting degrees when they should be seeking certifications or they obtain certifications when they are in need of the education and experience of a degree.

Depending on what you are trying to accomplish in life will determine which is more applicable to you.

Another thing to consider is that you can do several different things with a degree that many fail to realize. You can come up with novel ideas of economic potential that could function as a sub-competency of your degree. Use your imagination.

Ex: if you become a manager at one organization—did you know that you could also be a manager in another organization of a different type? To things matter: experience and ability. Did you stay on the job long enough to gain the experience and while in that position did you demonstrate the ability to manage well.

Because of the fact that people obtain degrees in fields that don't last or are over populated already, organizations are willing to hire individuals who have degrees in other fields that don't apply to the particular job in question. This is a plus.

When money is an issue consider the following options:

1. Grants
2. Student loans
3. Part-time side jobs
4. Tech over Major colleges
5. Certifications over degrees
6. Online course over in-class instruction
7. And there is always the lottery; just saying

Even if your job requires little to no education, having more than the required standard will give you much more job security and self-worth in the long run.

You also have the option of applying for an internship/apprenticeship with a company with the intention of learning a new trade and means of income. Think outside the box. I'm not claiming that you can become a millionaire just because you have an education; I'm not saying you can't either.

Things to consider:

❖ You get to place a value on education depending on its usefulness to you
❖ Employers will do so on its usefulness to their company or organization
❖ Others could benefit from your education even if you haven't considered them

"Education is a sacrifice that many make; a privilege most of them take for granted."

C. Know your margin of error

By now you may be fed up with the drudgery of ensuring a successful transition for yourself. I know. However, if you persevere, there will be payoff enough.

Take a deep breath and understand you don't have to get everything right just because your past is public knowledge. Don't put so much pressure upon yourself if you don't have to.

"Humans and mistakes have a love—hate relationship. We love them when we learn our lesson; we hate them when we don't."

Vocab

Margin of error - The margin required in order to ensure safety

Burnout - Melt, break, or become otherwise unusable

Overcompensate - Make up for shortcomings or a feeling of inferiority by exaggerating good qualities; Make excessive corrections for fear of making an error

Underperform - Perform less well or with less success than expected;

Desperate - A state in which all hope is lost or absent; desperate recklessness

Rebound - A reaction to a crisis, setback or frustration; Return to a former condition

Safety - The state of being certain that adverse effects will not be caused by some agent under defined conditions

Mistake - A wrong action attributable to bad judgment, ignorance or inattention; an understanding of something that is not correct

When we don't know or fail to respect our margin of error in society, we will begin to orchestrate our own down fall. We tend to dramatize every mistake as a failure; making mountains out of molehills.

"It's not what mistakes take from us that matters most; it's what we take from them that makes all the difference."

At this stage of your transition it is alright to make mistakes. Because you will recognize them quicker and learn much more from them than you would have before.

You'll be certain that nothing drastic is going to come from your minor mistake. You need this confidence. Without it, failure is eminent.

When you make a mistake and translate it into a failure you will begin to over-compensate for a problem that is not existent. You will over use your resources and your energy in a way that results in burnout; mentally, emotionally, or otherwise. In this state you are useless both to the task at hand and the tasks yet to come.

Or you may feel helpless to do anything about your perceived failure and begin to underperform in regards to your ambitions. Don't do it.

Don't be desperate yet. There is still hope for you to rebound and make the best out of the situation.

Alright, so this margin that I am referring to is created by you; not society. Society doesn't know where you are trying to go or what you are aiming to do; you do. So, you set the standard.

What is your threshold? Both for pain and for success. Once determined, this will be your safety zone. That place where you know in your heart of hearts that whatever happens can be overcome as long as you have not been removed from this zone.

"Welcome mistakes and they will compensate you greatly; overreact to them and you'll find debt and defeat."

D. Tell the tale and inspire others

How does it feel to rise from the ashes and reclaim everything you gave up through your crime? What is it like to be able to spread the wisdom of getting out and staying out of prison? How would you describe the impact that your successful transition has had on your family, friends, employers, and the community?

It's time to express this to others who find themselves where you used to be: in prison or headed there because of unprincipled living.

Vocab

Inspire - Supply the inspiration for; Serve as the inciting cause of; Fill with revolutionary ideas

Advocate - Speak, plead, or argue in favor of; Push for something

Catalyst – Something/someone that causes an important event to happen

When was the last time you sat under someone lecturing and said, "Man, he really gets it." or "I've never heard it put that way before?"

Do you remember what that was like? How it made you feel in the moment or the action it spurred you to? Wouldn't you want others to feel that same intoxication of inspiration?

There is only one you. Yes, other people have committed your type of crime; however, no one will tell your story like you. No one can reach the people you can reach. In laymen's terms no one can do your part. So, as they say in prison—*you do it!*

Everyone isn't here to reach a thousand people; nevertheless, each of us have at least one person only we can reach, guide, or motivate unto better. You may already know your one; you may not. Tell your story anyway and see what happens.

When it comes to inspiring others to do the same or better, the catalyst is in the details. Typically, you won't change people by telling them what they already know about you. Tell the masses what they are failing to see; what they have yet to realize about your reality.

Some of us caught our time and maxed it out without even giving it a second thought to how it changed us. So, if this is you, take time to reflect on it now. Put this workbook down, close your eyes, take a few deep breaths, and just watch the scenes of incarceration go by in slow motion. If you didn't learn something before—learn something now. It wasn't for not.

Where do you tell such a story? Well it depends. Where would you make the most impact?

- Boys/girls group homes
- DJJ
- SCDC or other Correction Depts.

- Transition houses
- Neighborhood Rec centers
- Allowing high schools or Alt. schools

Picture your prospective audience in your mind's eye: their age range, ethnicity, potential of ending up in prison or the grave. Now in the space provided below write the speech that you would deliver to that audience.

Title:____

Written by,

s/_________________________________

Workbook Glossary

Glossary

Abuse - Change the inherent purpose or function of something; Use wrongly, improperly or excessively;

Acceptance - A disposition to tolerate or accept people or situations; the mental attitude that something is believable and should be accepted as true

Addition - A component that is added to something to improve it; something added to what you already have;

Advocate - Speak, plead, or argue in favor of; Push for something

Agency - An administrative unit of government; the state of serving as an official and authorized delegate or agent; how a result is obtained or an end is achieved

Allowances - A permissible difference; allowing some freedom to move within limits

Appease - Cause to be more favorably inclined; gain the good will of; overcome or allay; Make peace with

At stake - In question or at issue; to be won or lost; at risk

Attest - Provide evidence for; stand as proof of; show by one's behavior, attitude, or external attributes; authenticate, affirm to be true, genuine, or correct, as in an official capacity;

Bad blood - A feeling of ill will arousing active hostility

Balance - Equality of distribution; harmonious arrangement or relation of parts or elements within a whole

Barrier - A structure or object that impedes free movement; any condition that makes it difficult to make progress or to achieve an objective; anything serving to maintain separation by obstructing vision or access

Behavior – the aggregate of the responses, reactions or movements made by an organism in any situation; The action or reaction of something under specified circumstances

Bridge - A structure that allows people…to cross an obstacle…

Burnout - Melt, break, or become otherwise unusable

Catalyst – Something/someone that causes an important event to happen

Certification - Confirmation that some fact or statement is true through the use of documentary evidence; validating the authenticity of something or someone

Character - A characteristic property that defines the apparent individual nature of something; the inherent complex of attributes that determines a person's moral and ethical actions and reactions

Citizen - A native or naturalized member of a state or other political community.

Cognitive dissonance - psychological conflict resulting from incongruous beliefs and attitudes held simultaneously.

Collective - Done by or characteristic of individuals acting together

Compensation - a defense mechanism that conceals your undesirable shortcomings by exaggerating desirable behaviors

Consequence - The outcome of an event especially as relative to an individual

Consider - Judge or regard; look upon; regard or treat with consideration, respect, and esteem

Consistency - Logical coherence and accordance with the facts

Context - The set of facts or circumstances that surround a situation or event

Continuity - Uninterrupted connection or union

Credibility - The quality of being believable or trustworthy

Curb - Lessen the intensity of; temper; hold in restraint; hold or keep within limits; to put down by force or authority; Place restrictions on.

Declassify – to lift the restriction on and make available again (or for the first time)

Desperate - A state in which all hope is lost or absent; desperate recklessness

Dimensional atrophy – weakening or deprivation of one's attribution dimensions due to lack of use or over use in one are over the others

Disadvantage - The quality of having an inferior or less favorable position; a flaw or weak point

Displace - Cause to move, usually with force or pressure; Take the place of or have precedence over; Cause to move or shift into a new position or place, both in a concrete and in an abstract sense

Doubt - The state of being unsure of something; Uncertainty about the truth, factuality or existence of something

Employable - Physically and mentally capable of working at a regular job and available

Estimate - The classification of someone or something with respect to its worth; an expert estimation of the quality, quantity, and other characteristics of someone or something

Example - A task performed or problem solved in order to develop skill or understanding; something/someone to be imitated

Excel - Distinguish oneself

Experience - The accumulation of knowledge or skill that results from direct participation in events or activities; be subject to, have the experience of

Forethought - Planning or plotting in advance of acting; Judiciousness in avoiding harm or danger

Forget - Dismiss from the mind; stop remembering;

Forgiveness - Compassionate feelings that support a willingness to forgive. The act of excusing a mistake or offense.

Germaneness - Pertinence by virtue of a close relation to the matter at hand

Goal (s) - The state of affairs that a plan is intended to achieve and that (when achieved) terminates the behavior intended to achieve it; the place designated as the end (as of a race or journey)

Guilt - The state of having committed an offense. Remorse caused by feeling responsible for some offense

Healthy - Promoting health; healthful. Exercising or showing good judgment.

Hindsight - Understanding the nature of an event after it has happened

History - The continuum of events occurring in succession leading from the past to the present and even into the future; All that is remembered of the past as preserved in writing; a body of knowledge

Hybrid: A composite of mixed origin

Impressionable - Easily impressed or influenced

Individual - Being or characteristic of one particular part of many; separate and distinct from others of the same kind; characteristic of or meant for a single person or thing; concerning one person exclusively

Influence - The effect of one thing (or person) on another; A power to affect persons or events especially power based on prestige etc.

Initiative - Readiness to embark on bold new ventures;

Inspire - Supply the inspiration for; Serve as the inciting cause of; Fill with revolutionary ideas

Intern - A student who works (often without pay) in order to gain experience

Investigate - Conduct an inquiry or investigation of

Lawful - Having a legally established claim; Authorized, sanctioned by, or in accordance with law.

Leverage - Strategic advantage; power to act effectively

Limitation - A principle that limits the extent of something; an act of limiting or restricting (as by regulation)

Location - A determination of the place where something/someone is

Margin of error - The margin required in order to ensure safety

Multi-focus – the ability to concentrate one's attention or give special emphasis to more than one object or area

Mutualism - The relation between two different species of organisms that are interdependent; each gains benefits from the other

Novel - Original and of a kind not seen before; pleasantly new or different

Overcompensate - Make up for shortcomings or a feeling of inferiority by exaggerating good qualities; Make excessive corrections for fear of making an error

Perception - A way of regarding situations or topics etc. The appearance of things relative to one another as determined by their distance from the viewer

Persuasive - Intended or having the power to induce action or belief

Priorities - Status established in order of importance or urgency

Probability - A measure of how likely it is that some event will occur; a number expressing the ratio of favorable cases to the whole number of cases possible; The quality of being probable; a probable event or the most probable event

Progress - Gradual improvement, growth or development; the act of moving forward (as toward a goal)

Purge - The act of clearing yourself (or another) from some stigma or charge. An act of removing by cleansing; ridding of sediment or other undesired elements.

Rapport - A relationship of mutual understanding or trust and agreement between people

Rebound - A reaction to a crisis, setback or frustration; Return to a former condition

Reclassify - Classify anew, change the previous classification

Reconciliation - The reestablishing of cordial relations. Getting two things to correspond.

Re-establish - Restoration to a previous state

Rehab - The restoration of someone to a useful place in society; vindication of a person's character and the re-establishment of that person's reputation

Rehabilitate - Help to readapt, as to a former state of health or good repute. Restore to a state of good condition or operation.

Reinforcement - An act performed to strengthen approved behavior.

Replace - Put in the place of another; switch seemingly equivalent items; Take the place or move into the position of; Substitute a person or thing for (another that is broken or inefficient or lost or no longer working or yielding what is expected)

Reputation - Notoriety for some particular characteristic; the general estimation that the public has for a person

Request - Express the need or desire for; ask for; Ask (a person) to do something; Inquire for (information)

Requirements - Something that is required in advance

Resilient - Recovering readily from adversity, depression, or the like

Resolve - Understand the meaning of; Reach a decision; Reach a conclusion after a discussion or deliberation; Bring to an end; come to a final conclusion

Responsibility - A form of trustworthiness; the trait of being answerable to someone for something or being responsible for one's conduct;

Restore - Restore by replacing a part or putting together what is torn or broken

Role model - Someone worthy of imitation

Sacrifice - Sell at a loss

Self-worth - The quality of being worthy of esteem or respect

Standard - A basis for comparison; a reference point against which other things can be evaluated; the ideal in terms of which something can be judged.

Stimulus - Make someone or something act in a particular way or do a particular thing;

excite the feelings or emotions of; disturb the peace of; provide the needed stimulus for

Summation - the process whereby multiple stimuli can produce a response...that one stimulus alone does not produce

Support system - A network of facilities and people who interact and remain in informal communication for mutual assistance; a network that enables you to live in a certain style

Tendency - A characteristic likelihood of or natural disposition toward a certain condition or character or effect; an attitude of mind especially one that favors one alternative over others

Transparency - The quality of being clear and transparent

Tunnel vision - Visual impairment involving a loss of peripheral vision

Underperform - Perform less well or with less success than expected;

Usage - Accepted or habitual practice; the amount or manner in which something is used or consumed

Veracity - The quality of being truthful; The quality of being correct, true, or close to the true value; Unwillingness to tell lies

Vindication - The act of vindicating or defending against criticism or censure etc.

Will - A fixed and persistent intent or purpose

Work History – a record that depicts all past, current, and ongoing occupations for which you received payment (Often used to determine employment risk, employee commitment level, and wages)

Extras

Refuse to doubt your ability to succeed

List below the five most important things you have taken from your incarceration:

1. ____
   ____
   ____
   ____.

2. ____
   ____
   ____
   ____.

3. ____
   ____
   ____
   ____.

4. ____
   ____
   ____
   ____.

5. ____
   ____
   ____
   ____.

Hold on to these lessons learned. They will surely be a guide to you during your transition and rehabilitation in society. Be sure to exhibit the experience you've gained to others so that they won't have to be incarcerated to learn the lessons.

If you had the opportunity to speak to your future self, ten years from today—what would you say? Would you compliment on the fine job over the years? Or would you scold yourself for not sticking to the plan?

In the space below you are given a chance to have that conversation. Have it in regards to where you want to be in ten years; not your current situation. Be specific to each area of your life: son, father, husband, mentor, citizen, religion, etc. If you don't worry about the details now, they may come back to haunt you in your future.

You will be able to look at this letter as time goes by to see if you have made yourself proud or regretful.

Dear future self

____

____

____

____

____

____

____

____

____ .

____

____

____

____

____

____

____

____

____ .

____

____

____

____

____

____

____

____ .

Sincerely,

My present self

Notes

About the author

Travis Abercrombie still resides in South Carolina with his three beautiful children: Unique, Sierra, and Travis Jr. He is an active member of the churches of Christ. He continues to reach out to the many men and women who are still incarcerated in SCDC and is currently developing his non-profit, Resurgence Post-conviction Rehabilitation Program (*RP*^{2}).